Mass Media in a Mass Society

To our family, with love

Mass Media in a Mass Society

Myth and Reality

RICHARD HOGGART

continuum
LONDON • NEW YORK

Continuum

The Tower Building
11 York Road
London SE1 7NX

15 East 26th Street
New York
NY 10010

www.continuumbooks.com

First published 2004

British Library Cataloguing-in-Publication Data
A catalogue record for this book is available from the British Library.

ISBN 0-8264-7285-0 (Hardback)

Typeset by Kenneth Burnley, Wirral, Cheshire.
Printed and bound by Cromwell Press Ltd, Trowbridge, Wilts.

Contents

Acknowledgements

The books by most of the authors quoted here are out of copyright.

The few quotations from modern authors are so small as to fall well within normally accepted limits for this kind of book. I am of course glad to acknowledge here those authors (or executors) and publishers.

The authors are: W. H. Auden, Saul Bellow, Isaiah Berlin, John Betjeman, T. S. Eliot, E. M. Forster, Lord Goodman, Graham Greene, Tony Harrison, Geoffrey Hill, Philip Larkin, Edwin Muir, Iris Murdoch, George Orwell, Ezra Pound, J. B. Priestley, Lord Reith, George Steiner, R. H. Tawney, Dylan Thomas and W. B. Yeats.

Work on a book such as this requires the general consulting of many books from many publishers. I owe a debt to the following publishers and journals: Bloomsbury, *British Journalism Review,* Cambridge University Press, Cassell, Chambers, Faber and Faber, Fraser-Stewart, Longman, *Granta,* Oxford University Press, Penguin, *Private Eye,* Routledge (and, at times, with Kegan Paul), *Times Literary Supplement* (and Derwent May), Wordsworth and Yale University Press (and Fred Inglis).

I owe, once more, a great debt to Geoffrey Goodman, Stephen Hearst, John Miller and Roy Shaw for their very helpful readings of the typescript; to Stephen Jones for technical guidance at each stage; and to Marilyn Jones for going on keeping track.

Mike Shaw and Jonathan Pegg at Curtis Brown were, as always, indispensable.

As was Robin Baird-Smith and all at Continuum.

Finally, again as so often, my thanks to all the family and, in particular, to my wife Mary.

R. H.

Introduction

Like many discursive books, this one proved to have an overall shape partly hidden even from the author until it was completed.

Imagine a wide and deep river flowing towards the sea and at its estuary dividing into several interconnecting channels. The river may be thought of as carrying the vast body of intellectual disputation and social change which has occurred over at least the last century and a half. The channels are important aspects of our present individual and collective lives which have been fed by the main flood.

Here, we are chiefly examining only one of those channels: that concerning the mass media in the mass society, which can also be called the communications, consumer, commodity, populist or relativist society.

So, Chapter One sets out as economically as possible some of those elements towards change which the river has fed into its channels. For the emerging mass society those elements include declining religious belief, democratic institutions – both developing and challenged – advanced technology, increasing prosperity, and so on.

Other chapters examine the results of those changes. Thus, Chapter Two describes the new servants of mass society, Chapter Three outlines cardinal features of that society, and Chapter Four two of its main 'icons' (to use one of its own favourite words). Chapter Five examines broadcasting, the overwhelmingly most important form of communication, which has developed so as to mirror and influence the new society. The remaining chapters discuss the effects of these forces, beginning with their impact on language, and ending with suggestions for confronting the worst of their effects.

This book aims to gather together and develop some of the ideas on social change about which I have written over half a century. Nothing is said directly, however, about two increasingly important issues of more recent years: globalization and the environment. They would have required vastly extra space but, more importantly for my purposes, they only marginally enter the thoughts of most people; as the exponents of mass communications know.

RICHARD HOGGART

'Kindness and courage can repair Time's faults,
And serving him breeds patience and courtesy
In us, light sojourners and passing subjects.'

(Edwin Muir, 'The Good Town')

'The greatest thing a human soul ever does
in this world is to see something, and tell what
he saw in a plain way . . .'

(John Ruskin, *Modern Painters*)

Chapter 1

Mass Society: An Outline

'Forward, forward let us range,
Let the great world spin for ever down the ringing grooves
of change.'

(Tennyson, 'Locksley Hall')

The advantages of mass communications seem obvious and we all
know them. Or think we do. But often those convictions mistake
the tool for its objective. If the objective is undesirable, not
worthwhile, then the tool – the conduit – is not worthwhile
either, it is misused. This is true no matter how amazingly
advanced and sophisticated some of these developments may
seem to us, the first generation to have them.

Mass communications can be invaluable. They can help to save
lives, through accelerating the use of rescue services, for
example, or through the invention of a great range of electronic
medical devices and so on; from helping to keep airplanes in the
sky and ships safe at sea, to developing almost instantaneous
communication across the globe.

Given other characteristics and forces within this kind of
society, some ultra-fast forms of communication may inevitably
be being put to other than worthwhile purposes. But the widespread use of mass communications is inevitable between free
societies, as the rapid spread of mobile phones amply illustrates.

A great deal of these types of contact devices are valuable in industry and commerce, in times of an individual's need, or simply to keep in touch better with family, friends and acquaintances. All these gains apply chiefly to the 'developed' world, of course, and, even within that world, hardly to the un-possessed.

Do mass communications in themselves and, as it were, intrinsically, 'help us to understand one another better', and so reduce, most importantly, the dangers of small or large conflicts? A popular myth is that they can, or will, do such things. Yet greater knowledge may just as easily lead to greater dislike – to know all is not to forgive all. The ready accessibility of information of all types does not almost automatically and insensibly lead to greater comprehension of ourselves and our world. Information is in itself inert. It may lead to knowledge only if it has been considered, ordered, assessed. Does knowledge lead inevitably to the acquisition of wisdom? Certainly not. Well-informed and knowledgeable people may be lacking in wisdom, which may come above all from disinterested and thoughtful reflection; an illiterate person may become wise from experience. Mass communication in any form cannot ineluctably lead from information to knowledge to wisdom. T. S. Eliot was right when he asked where was the wisdom we have lost in knowledge [and] where the knowledge we have lost in information? Geoffrey Hill put the question more pawkily: 'In what sense or senses is the computer acquainted with original sin?' Information and knowledge may, if a particular individual is willing, somewhat ease the progress towards wisdom. No more.

The Basic Agents of Change

The break-up – the slow but uninterrupted dissolution – of old beliefs, assumptions and habits; the reduction of the sense of different social placings and of the *authority* which sustained them are prime agents of change – at all levels but most markedly below the middle-class, because that is where they are bearing most widely, where for good or ill they are most felt. A middle-class person might habitually have resented the airs of a flagrant snob, but had the compensation of knowing that there were others on an even lower rung. The new forces seem on the whole more egalitarian; they affect almost all of us.

The Loss of Belief
These forces were brought about by an unusually rapid coming together over at least a century and a half of sustained intellectual criticism of existing assumptions and beliefs, especially the religious. There followed the filtered transmission of these seismic ideas downwards and outwards via 'gate-keepers' and other intermediaries, from neighbours and workmates through to print in its various forms. Thence through the airwaves, first via radio and then through the most important influence so far – television. It would be difficult but worthwhile to try to assess and compare the different degrees of influence exerted by face-to-face peer-groups at work or in pubs and other meeting places, as compared with that exercised by journals, especially popular newspapers, and by broadcasting. Some will be diluted, some inevitably misinterpreted. It seems likely that, in first recognizing these changes and especially in putting names to them, the print and on-air journalists were the bellwethers, and more important than face-to-face influencers. Yet that is only an impression; face-to- face persuasion may, in the long run, be more effective.

The last half-century in particular has seen the *decline of religious belief* gain speed, its irrelevance become more widely and firmly accepted as an apparently simple matter of fact. Especially among younger people, space exploration has no doubt hastened the process. There are many indicators, in addition to the loss of church and chapel attendances. It is indicated as always in favourite idioms, such as those which reveal ethical face-saving in response to the sense of ultra-existential loss: 'I'm not a believer or churchgoer, but I do have my rules (or some such) . . . '; or even: 'But I do believe in Christian ethics,' moving on to assured and explicit renunciations and occasional replacements. Two markers, chosen almost casually and only twenty years apart, illustrate the speed of change in widespread, explicit attitudes. In 1963, *Honest to God,* by John Robinson, Bishop of Woolwich, was castigated for undermining belief. It would cause hardly a stir today. Twenty years ago, only two decades after Robinson, Bishop Jenkins' questioning of the literal truth of the Resurrection caused little more than a ripple in newspapers. Individual and social changes – in opinions and in varieties of taste more than in other areas – move unprecedentedly quickly nowadays, as we shall see in several contexts later. All of us are affected, so it is as well to bear in mind from the start that we cannot fairly shake our heads over what seem unfortunate new attitudes adopted by others without also considering their effects on ourselves. But, whatever the changes, we are almost all of us still more extensively and firmly influenced by old-style class and class-education, in our responses to change, than we always wish to recognize.

As to the *decline of authority,* church and chapel were traditionally the main sources of authority, and to some extent the Church of Rome remains influential. Most of us are left in – not necessarily stranded in – a much broader, more open and, above all, more *self-choosing world*; without the old ethical compasses for our behaviour towards both ourselves and others. At first this might seem not only to the good but entirely to the good. Later, we will need to look critically at these effects across several areas.

Self-choosing
Yet self-choosing has its prices, some of them high; but these are largely ignored or extensively explained away. This is a world with even more powerful and insistent, yet often as if subcutaneous, new indicators. Self-choosing is influenced almost inescapably by

4

newly offered choices from newer and immensely enhanced forms of persuasion and increased numbers of sophisticated persuaders. The progress is: discard or adopt old habits > adapt > reinforce > add the new. This process first reinforces those older attitudes which suit the new world's new purposes; second, it discourages those which do not now suit; and, third, it encourages new and more suitable styles – suitable to its own ends. All these different patterns of attitudes meet some resistances, as – to take a slightly colourful but not greatly important instance – in various forms of Evangelicanism in the Church of England, especially of the 'Happy Clappy' type.

For the religious sense is not easily lost. It would be tempting to suggest that the exhibitions by members of the public after Princess Diana's death, and those after the murder of two ten-year-old girls in mid-2002, were so strong because they were substitutes for the loss of formal religious manifestations. This, too, requires fuller attention later. The idea may certainly be worth pursuing; but first the enquirer would have to try to assess the contribution of the mass media to each of those responses, the degree of personal, directly felt emotion and the extent to which it was encouraged by the mass media.

There are many reasons why the diminution or removal of those main outside pillars of authority can be welcomed. In principle, self-choosing seems preferable, but is not easily arrived at or lived with, especially since it is discouraged by many other and often new kinds of pseudo-authority, the authority wielded by those apparently innocent, those wooingly winning – rather than explicitly and traditionally authorized or qualified – persuaders. Of these, two main and intertwined groups are native to would-be democracies: those of the *populists* and the *levellers*. Essentially, they promote not individual choice and decision-making ('Here I stand. I can do no other.') but communitarianism, which is a debased form of community spirit. Effective self-choosers divide, in some things stand outside the main desirable large groupings; and are bad for business.

One of the main losses is the widespread corruption of language, its use not to carry the free explorations and transmission of intellect and imagination but to make those qualities subject to exploitation for persuasion. The interested aim dominates, rarely the disinterested; with the pursuit of money or power (often disguised) as the over-riding goals. Available money is to be used chiefly for the mass pursuit of that which pleases, which involves the encouragement of narrowly defined attitude-changing and so fits the main drives.

Of such people the 'purest' examples are those City types whose antics have for two decades fascinated the newspaper columnists, because of their huge salaries, their large annual bonuses, and their 'champagne lifestyle' in a succession of fashionable bars and cars. They are not themselves active persuaders but are prime examples of the kind of life to which mass persuasion points; the admired end of the line, the extreme behavioural point of societies in which it is assured, to those who can exploit it, that the right attitude for them is that everything, even happiness, can be bought; and who therefore, it is almost unnecessary to say, worship money. They are the younger 'filthy-rich', but un-rooted, detached from local communities, held within a world of their own kind, psychologically suspended somewhere over the City.

And all for making no useful thing nor adding anything to the sum of human knowledge; simply the cute, no doubt the clever, pushing around of invisible money. To paraphrase D. H. Lawrence: 'never a real or a true thing said' – or done. This recalls also Swift's dismissal in *Gulliver's Travels* – of politicians, but it will serve well here: 'Whoever could make two ears of corn or two blades of grass to grow upon a spot of ground where only one grew before, would deserve better of mankind, and do more essential service to his country than the whole race of politicians put together.'

Attitudes Towards Sexual Matters

Not all persuasions towards change are meretricious or explored only by commercial persuaders. Sometimes the latter are climbing on a bus which other forces, perhaps less interested, have set in motion; they then usually increase its speed and extend its destination-board. So we would do well to start with a change which, on balance (and though many people would not agree here), may be regarded as a gain: Partnership.

The most striking and visible example of current psychological and social change under the impact of forces already described has been the acceptance of *partnership* in place of marriage, quietly but extensively at all or almost all levels. This is most surprising in that it is to be found in that part of the old working-class which seemed most set in its belief in marriage. Such people have not, though – or not yet – adopted, as have many higher up the class-ladder, a roughly concurrent greater freedom in speech, especially sexual. Language historically regarded as vulgar and unsayable; e.g. 'fuck', remains out of bounds. In the respectable working-class, that is; many men in heavy industry have long found it difficult to utter a sentence without that loading.

The move to partnership and away from marriage was accomplished with remarkably little resistance, perhaps chiefly because of the arrival of the contraceptive pill. The change was rapid and widespread; other forces had been at work to make the pill acceptable, notably some of those now being listed. The pill, it seems likely, came on cue and accelerated the change. A related gain is the removal of such words as 'bastard' and 'illegitimate' from the official vocabulary

The recognition of *homosexuality* and *lesbianism* by many people lay betwixt and between; between language not much broadened or vulgarized and the acceptance of what used simply to be called 'living in sin'. It is characteristic of older working-class attitudes to men and to women that homosexuality and lesbianism were approached differently. Homosexuality was recognized but with its own insulting labels, such as: 'pansy', 'nancy boy', 'ponce', 'queer' or 'poof'. I do not remember a single acknowledgement of lesbianism, or any cant word of dismissal for it. An aunt of mine lived, from when she was in her thirties, with another woman, until the latter died many years later. If we had tried to guess why, we would have said that they had similar characters, both probably 'put off' by the thought of sex and tending to think of men as big, clumsy, demanding and often boozy creatures. They spat the word 'sex' as though they were ejecting a dirty frog; a nasty experience and against 'proper' nature. Oddly, they could be slightly skittish with men when briefly in a safe environment.

Prosperity

The next main agent is that greater *prosperity*, which has been diffused at almost all levels (not to the 'underclass' whose inhabitants, in relative and sometimes real terms, are often worse off than their grandparents were). Far more and far greater ranges of people have, and have very quickly, become used to spare money in the pocket, money to use freely at the end of the week or month; discretion, room to manoeuvre; to *spend* – an example of the positive side of the Micawber axiom. Since this is new to a great swathe, probably a majority, of the population, it can seem a sort of liberation ('I'm spoiled for choice'). Not, though, in itself a new kind of pleasure, this spending; the difference is in regularity, scope and volume. Spending too much and with money needed for the home had made 'spend-thrift' a severe and much used epithet. But working-class people have always loved 'looking round the market' on Saturday afternoons and spending what if anything they could afford; just walking around and looking can be enjoyable. Remember the delight of Mrs Morel in buying her bits of pottery, cheap, from a stall, and showing them off to Paul, in *Sons and Lovers*? Typical. The huge covered market in Leeds is a magnet for people from miles around. My late sister did not have a comfortable 'going on' but loved that market. Late in life, she recalled that in the early days of marriage they had wandered through Leeds market and 'Jack saw a lovely sort of Chinese tea set and bought it for me'. The contrast between that touching little incident and the years which followed was painful. It is easy to understand the attraction of the big, cornucopia supermarkets, especially those which display little social 'side' and simply 'pile it high'.

Regular, habitual, shopping in shops rather than markets, was greatly enjoyed by many Victorian and Edwardian women of the middle-class but could not extend much further down. Even by the end of the last century, being excited by the seasonal sales started in the lower-middle not the working-class. To take advantage of them, you needed spare money in hand or with a bank or building society.

That pattern is still to be found today in both the 'underdeveloped' and 'developing' world; as in, for instance, Brazil. The marked differences between shops there and, more strikingly, the lines of passengers embarking on many a 747 leaving Sao Paulo in the evening for Paris or Lisbon, illustrates this; from top to bottom, and particularly through the women who board in each class. Some sweep up into the First Class section, going for the pleasures of fashionable shopping; others, in Economy, are going to take up domestic labour in strange lands.

The change today with working-class people is, then, of scale, the sense not always and necessarily of an excess but certainly of more to spend, probably much more, than their parents and grandparents had; the freedom to choose, to decide for themselves, to 'branch out'. At present the pinnacles or major signals of this change, and main agents towards the melding of old class differences, are the enormous shopping malls such as Bluewater and Meadowhall (what throwback romanticism in titles). Icons of Consumer Globalization. Those really do move towards creating the sense of a cornucopia, a global cornucopia since many of the stores belong to national or international conglomerates and so their offerings are almost predictable from place to place, continent to continent. If all this works, then, in spite of their huge rents, profits will emerge.

The same is true of the fast-food outlets. Most of their offerings reflect the dead centre of popular taste, which has proved in these things almost universal. In general, they do not greatly attract middle-class or middle-brow adults, or those even higher socially. There are inevitably some exceptions, especially among children – and some aristocrats.

These entrepreneurs of clothing or food and much else know their targets and in general how to hit them; including knowing when taste is about to change, or needs a push to make people look favourably at, and take up a new and, for their outlets, financially promising style. In the developed or near-developed world they are learning also how to straddle classes at the same time and place; Tesco's promotions are good examples of that both in Britain and in, for example, Bratislava. This whole phenomenon and practice remains solidly rooted in that widely spread and historic love of shopping and, now, the ability for it to flower as never before across the majority of a population.

Technology

Technology moves to meet those needs; and today technology moves at ever-increasing speeds; changes in taste, in some important respects, keep in step. The latest and one of the most unexpectedly rapid examples is the adoption of mobile phones. It seems hardly to have gone through the usual phases, moving in acceptance through different levels of acquisition by class, occupation or even geography. Only a few years ago it would have been extremely rare to see housewives obviously belonging to what used to be called 'the working-class', who on their way round a huge supermarket, would pause as some odd thought or question struck them, and then take a mobile phone out of their handbags and dial home, or even to their husbands at work if they are able to take calls. That is now commonplace.

It in turn recalls an earlier and similar example: the adoption of television. Commercial decisions on how many televisions would be needed in the first few years were influenced by the assumption that sets, being costly, would initially be bought chiefly by those above the working-class. That was mistaken on two counts: it underestimated the early disdain for 'the goggle box' among many middle-class people and above; it under-estimated also the working-class willingness to buy something which would give pleasure, even if, on a 'sensible' assessment, it could not be afforded. 'The never-never', hire-purchase, solved that problem; and raised others.

A much more important example of the influence of new tech-nology – this time the term is used to include scientific research whose outcome has a powerful direct impact on a majority of the population – is the appearance of the contraceptive pill, noted earlier. It was approved by the American Food and Drug Agency in 1960, and by the mid-sixties was spreading through the devel-oped world at all social levels. The growing spirit of self-choosing, with the declining power of external advisers, and emerging widespread prosperity were, as in so much else, the main agents of change here.

Pervasive Capitalism
Most powerfully affecting of all the above changes, helping to decide what falls away, what stays and what newly succeeds – like an enormous partly subterranean engine moving across and behind our whole living-space – is the fact of *capitalism*. We live in a democracy or, better, a putative or would-be democracy; a democracy with some though not always explicit constraining terms on the acceptance of – the living with – capitalism. It is professedly though not always actually 'open', in that it is not centralized and ordered in a totalitarian manner. It believes in

freedom of speech and to some degree manages to practise that.

Capitalism, within this mixed system, is generally accepted (though not generally praised), and successful because it is rooted in an almost universal instinct: to amass wealth, to 'get on', to be at the top of the heap. This instinct is virtually as strong as that which, in Britain at least, urges you to help your neighbour.

Ours can more fairly be called an open commercial (again, 'would-be') democracy, in which the market is in many respects paramount though not all powerful. This, we tell ourselves with some justice, encourages initiative and discourages direction from an official centre, which so often proves to be crippling, whether fascist or communist. We have had overwhelmingly bad examples of both those in the last half-century. With all its limitations a more or less open, capitalist, more or less democratic, form may be, again we often tell ourselves, the least worst, not – since that does not, and may never, exist, though we should go on striving for it – the best type of society. Hidden in that often unsavoury confusion there are some useful truths, especially as to our degree of individual freedom, and our understanding of the ways in which that may be being perverted. If capitalism were to be entirely happy working within a professed 'democracy', then probably the constraints on it would be inadequate.

We remind ourselves less than we should that that freedom includes others' freedom to con, corral, cheat us as they ride effectively on the capitalist spume at all levels. The public relations practitioners and advertising agents, in particular, subvert the language so as to sustain their false claims as to the definition and reality of their picture of a desirable social and personal life. We fail to recognize the true inadequacy, indeed awfulness but nevertheless force, of the capitalist bosses' favourite maxims, such as 'I owe it to my shareholders' (used to justify many a shifty practice). The verb 'to owe' is shifty there, too; in normal use it can mean the acknowledgment of a plain debt of money, or it can indicate an ethical responsibility – 'I owe it to my family to . . .'. Set against those two, 'I owe it to my shareholders' is revealed as pseudo-pious. More direct, from its closed, self-justifying world, is: 'But it's a *business* decision.' There is also: 'That's all very well . . . but what's the bottom line? My job is to maximize profits,' and: 'No. That's not in my commercial interest' (blunt recognitions of the profit motive as the final arbiter). Perhaps the worst is: 'I charge what the market will bear.' A haulier was revealed on television as greatly overcharging – exploiting – farmers during the foot and mouth disaster. He showed no shame and merely replied, as if quoting the Bible: 'Of course, I charge what the market will bear.' From the buyers' side, '*Caveat emptor*' is rarely uttered but stands silently behind these and all such mottoes. At a lower level we have 'There's one born every minute' (a happy acceptance of practising deceit before the innocent), 'rip-offs', 'scams' and 'fiddles'. In 2001 British Gas charged a minimum of £97 plus parts for a call-out, unless you had been knowing enough to take out their annual insurance, which many people cannot afford anyway. At this point one always recalls the late Cecil King's notorious but sadly confessional statement, to the effect that only those who run popular newspapers know just how gullible, how low in educated understanding, are most English people.

The capitalists' and some right-wing politicians' favourite pious, misleading myth is that which claims that the greater the profit made at the top, the more of it filters steadily down to the rest. Tell that to the underclass, or to the millionaires of the City caught in an off-guard moment; that weak insincere wish employed to hide a real distortion. The filtering-down expresses itself in the proliferation of cheap labour used in their homes and elsewhere.

The bottom level was well illustrated by a solicitor recently interviewed on television about his representing a couple who, though they might have had some legal right on their side, had nevertheless and plainly acted wickedly, immorally (if those two adverbs are recognized) towards those they were pursuing. The solicitor's answer, given in an entirely assured tone, was to the effect: 'Yes. I know it could be called "immoral", but that is not an element I can take into account professionally.' It seems likely that some other solicitors would find nothing objectionable in that answer, nothing which challenged their professional consciences. Nor would many in commerce or, for that matter, many Trade Union officials when they are defending a member whose case is, ethically, thoroughly unpleasant and smelly. Such long-standing methods come straight from capitalist practice and move the more easily into the relativist world.

These strictures on capitalism will cause offence to some, perhaps many. They will insist that there are some 'decent' capitalists, given to charitable enterprises and fair-dealing. Agreed; and there are plenty of hired voices to make, or over-make, those saving and respectable points for them. Such attitudes can and do exist within the body of capitalism but they are in a minority. Usually their shareholders, assuming that, perhaps for P.R. purposes, they will accept such deviations by the management, will keep a close eye on them. They run against the natural impulses of capitalism, and in general those impulses will prevail, and the shareholders will try to ensure that they do; especially in societies where most journalists and other gate-keepers have not taken the measure of the endless struggle between those impulses and the urge towards an achieved democracy.

Class and Education

Two other important contributors to today's large, secular changes need to be introduced. They are, first, the *sense of class*. (To call it 'the class system' blurs the reality by smelling of conspiracy-theory. It is a pervasive fact, like a persistent fog, but not a system.) For almost a century there have been claims that 'class is dead'. That is not true but the nature and style of class-feeling have been changing, and the main forces in the emerging new society are helping that along; though not towards any condition which could accurately be called 'classless'. As we shall see, the persuaders are themselves guided partly by that false conviction, in pursuit of their own purposes; it does have profitable uses for them. Therefore, 'if society has really started to change, let's push change along' seems to be the unspoken – perhaps unrealized – attitude. A greater range of social changes which many of them also recognize and exploit is helping those ends too. They have to do with mutations in the sense of class; as new, still tripartite, social divisions emerge.

The second contributory factor is that we are a surprisingly *under-educated society* – surprising for one so advanced. This is odd when one recalls that just over a century ago we were one of the first nations to be able to claim that we had a substantially literate population. That was at a very low level and certainly not adequate to living in a complex, modern 'open democracy'. It is commonly claimed today that about fifteen per cent of the population are insufficiently literate, not able, for example, to make sense of even a common kind of printed instruction, and thus far less able to detect the deceptions in many an advertisement addressed to them. They exist at a level of near-literacy, one sufficient for them to be comprehensively deceived; more might make them more able to blow the gaff on the admen, and that would hardly do. Overall, the situation encourages exploitation. It is in the interest of the tycoons and their minions that many of us remain under-educated to that degree. It is also in their interest that almost all politicians in almost all parties do not begin to take the measure of this situation, here and now, as we enter a new century surrounded by yet more new instruments; many of which, paradoxically and depressingly, thrive on the existence of such an under-educated body of citizens.

It is true that technical illiteracy can exist in people of whom many may have learned shrewdness, possess 'native wit', some ability to see through several kinds of 'scam'. The success of many kinds of deception shows that to be a limited protective quality in the face of today's more sophisticated barrages. Call round a row of council houses in a poor district to find this proved, beginning by discovering how many owe more than they can pay back to several hire-purchase firms; and, of those, how many are already in hock to the loan-sharks who exploit and feed on their condition.

The spirit of class division and the educational system come together to reinforce this social divisiveness. Above all, the private schools – especially the public schools – continue to perpetuate these divisions. They train for exclusiveness, for privileged opportunities to enter Oxbridge, for the making of contacts towards the right sorts of profession and for much else. They make it more difficult for the state – the true 'public' sector – to realize our individual and collective potentials, educationally and socially. They reinforce the old class system and are re-inforcing its emerging successor. Again, some will object to this flat, hardly qualified assertion. Yes, there are a few exceptions and some partial exceptions, and some movements towards a more democratic spirit and its suitable institutions but, in general, the statement holds.

The brightest and some of the not-so-bright come out of Oxbridge each year knowing, just knowing, that their feet are destined to lead to London, the City, the press, broadcasting, the stock exchange, the law, the great international commercial and industrial enterprises. Their expectations are largely met. Those who prove inadequate can no longer be sent to govern New South Wales; they are likely to move into the newer fashion-accessory trades: upmarket restaurants, smart clubs, small chic hotels, posh health centres and expensive golf clubs.

English education has long trained for life on either the *escalator* or the *carousel*. Educated for the carousel, you continue going round and round at the same level, with few if any expectations. Some important modern forces work to strengthen that set of reductive and tenacious assumptions. This is the poverty of expectations at which Aneurin Bevan – 'lift your eyes!' – railed. Luckier people expect, and have access to, the escalator. Onward and upward.

There are now exceptions, forced upon such as, say, the City. They need people with exceptionally rapid reactions, able to handle enormous amounts of money in movement across the world. A new breed of meritocrats emerges, for whom class, family and school do not much count in the decision whether to appoint them.

It will be fiercely replied, to any argument against the freedom to pay for the education of one's children outside the state system, that such an argument is at bottom undemocratic. We should be able to spend our own hard-earned and taxed money in any reasonable way we choose, to buy better education rather than to go on fancy foreign holidays, have expensive cars and so on. On the face of it, that is a powerful argument and one which can be respected.

But you are buying not education in itself but education as a hoped-for tool towards giving your children an advantage as against children whose parents cannot afford to do likewise even if they wished to do so. You are helping from the start to continue and strengthen a divisiveness founded in part on greater educational and social opportunity. Viewed from this perspective, the argument for equality of educational *opportunity* from the start – differences of inherent potential will show soon enough – is of the same order as the argument that all citizens should have equality under the law, or access to clean water, or to the use of the National Health Service (though they are also distorted).

17

Equality of educational opportunity is then also seen as a universal right. I do not expect this argument to be generally accepted.

It is harder to object to those parents who argue that they have discovered mental limitations in their child and wish to reduce them. But for each of those there are very many for whom the decision to apply for a place at a public school, or to pay for extra tuition so that their child may gain a place at a local selective school, is guided by the dominant impulse to give them 'a head start' which must mean 'over others'.

There are other errors outside these great public areas of debate; now in some, too many, state schools. Most state schools are short of money for extra-curricular activities which can be of considerable value. Usually with success, private schools incorporate those costs into their basic fees or call on comfortably off parents. Along to the state school comes the representative of a soft-drinks firm and offers money if they are allowed to place their vending machines on the school's premises. Presumably, some Heads do not agree, out of an obvious principle. Some Heads agree, though rather unwillingly. Others see no grounds for objecting. Yet most soft drinks contain excessive amounts of sugar, of which many children get far too much in different ways out of school. It is one role of schools not to yield to proposals which increase unhealthy habits, no matter how much money such proposals may bring for the school's own good causes. Does the Department, now unhappily but typically labelled, 'for Education and Skills' advise schools on this? According to a recent rather on-the-one-hand-on-the-other article in a national weekly, the Department leaves the decision to individual Heads, which presumably leaves them with the impression that the Department has no strong feelings in such a matter, not a sense that this is so important an issue as to require at least a 'steer' from the national Department. That is very odd.

Inevitably, the practice widens. It has been reported (August, 2002) that in some schools the practice of providing a jug of water at each table in the canteen has been stopped, that children who want water have then to buy the bottled kind at the servery. If this is so, though it seems likely still to be rare, then it is certainly the point at which the Department should intervene. Children need water at lunchtime and should not be made to pay for it. The author of the essay noted above ended as she began, in a manner typical of the times: the drinks salesman was only doing his job, the schools do need more discretionary money, the Department is protecting the Heads' degree of independence. There was no sense of a further element in play at any level here, of a judgement which could be weighty and probably overriding. One almost heard at the end the usual rubric: 'And after all, who am I to judge?'

All this is a growing enterprise, known in the trade as Direct Marketing and particularly aimed, with samples and various kinds of trade-marked gifts, at eight to ten year olds. It is estimated that at present one in four schools is receptive. Another recent article on the phenomenon ends similarly to the one quoted just above: 'Some are beginning to wonder, however, whether such marketing is a wolf in sheep's clothing.' Well, I never!

Exploitation or Community

We remain a divided, not – which could be healthy – a diverse, society; we are a society moving towards a new or, by now, new-ish form of the old three-tiered divisions: minorities at top and bottom, with the persuaders' prime target, of about seventy-five per cent, in the middle. Against this background it is all the more necessary to recognize that, left to its own impulses, the practice of capitalism is – has to be – exploitative and therefore often immoral; all the rest is palliative – sticking-plaster. The big bosses are under constant pressure from competitors, here and abroad, who could and willingly would ruin their rivals' enterprises; and it often shows in their faces, notably the eyes, mouth and jaw.

There is certainly no sure art to find the mind's construction in the face. Yet of the dozen or so tycoons I have met only two or three looked, on duty, thoughtfully and sympathetically open – generally, they cannot afford to. Theirs has to be the rule of the accounts, of the bottom line, of the pressures of the shareholders. Those are the indelible spots on the leopard and no amount of well-intended and well-paid labour from outsiders or self-justifying scrubbing by the zoo's insiders can remove them. That is both the over-riding and the under-riding thrust. Even our society, which likes to pride itself on comfortably reigning in the worst excesses of capitalism, its 'unacceptable face', is riddled with corruption, from operators of many kinds who fiddle their clients and under-insure their workers, to City investment conmen. Our reigning ins, our checks and balances, are inadequate. And the higher the less adequate, especially since there are always plenty of solicitors and barristers who will for a suitable fee discover new modes of avoidance which could not exactly be called evasions; they will cheerfully try to insist that black is white.

It is in these areas a Hobbesian world, in which the Devil takes the hindmost, a 'stuff you, Jack, I'm alright' world. Why should it be otherwise if, increasingly, the only thing required from us is lip-service to morality, no sustaining ethic to challenge usury and promote charity. In such a world we complacently allow British workers to be sacked and as easily ignore that the goods we buy from the under-developed world are the products of sweated labour. This is 'one world' only in that lines do connect us – with those we exploit; as does most of the developed world. For many, morality is domestic; we are generous, even indulgent, to our families. That morality is switched off as we get into our cars and go to work each day.

So, though many big bosses have a guarded, watchful, determined expression, they do not look guilty. To feel that way, to admit it to themselves, would collapse the world around them. Better to have an expression in reserve, for public use; perhaps one of apparent good nature, or a cloak of aloofness.

Capitalism will not easily change its nature but may be alleviated in practice; much more than at present. To assist that process it would be as well if many more of us were aware of its sharp practices at different levels and in different areas, for its effects spread into almost all corners of society. One simple example is that almost all our newspapers are owned by people, for profit and perhaps to have influence; but certainly to make profit. Their journalists know this; and many know that, if they are not to endanger their jobs, they must commit distressing invasions of privacy so as to 'get a good story'. The Press Complaints Commission, to which people may refer since they cannot face in court a newspaper which could destroy them financially, sometimes pussy foots around since its composition ensures that its culture is that of many newspapers; of the press network in which the defensive justification of 'the public interest' is simply equated with 'what happens to interest the public' – whereas, in fact, those two are often wide apart; and should be. A prurient incident may well interest the public. It may not serve any conceivable public interest, but will serve rather the equally prurient interest assumed in most readers.

All this requires a firm and constant guard if we are ever to become a near-genuine open democracy. At this point one wonders whether such issues are raised in those expensive Schools of Business Administration here or, more often, in America. Perhaps – but as something for the birds?

Do those schools of journalism in British universities and further education colleges ask their students to face the ethical questions raised by their desired profession? From the answers recently given on the radio by a professor from one such school, it seems not. Somewhere underneath he was aware of this troubling issue. It was plain that his courses did not explicitly require the students to face this overwhelmingly important question. He admitted that it existed but insisted that above all what his students wanted was to become journalists and that he must do all in his power to train them for that, *as it is*. And the ethical questions? Having got a job, he added, they must examine their consciences if (!) ethical matters arose. Knowing that if they stood firm on such an issue against their editor's or proprietor's opinion they might soon be out of a job? Not to raise such questions seems a dereliction of duty in an academic at any level. Ethical questions abound within journalism yet apparently those who teach journalism can excuse themselves entirely from addressing these things. One supposes that the old excuse of 'living in the Real World' is hiding in the background there.

And yes, even today, our mixed and semi-blind society produces a more liveable space for most of us most of the time than would totalitarianism or any form of complete and assured ideology. We are in some ways stuck with it. But, again, it has to have its rapacious instincts controlled and its pious defences subjected to powerful and continuous batterings. Which is why we have – should have – a great variety of bodies, regulatory and official commissions or voluntary watch dogs, to protect us from the entwining tentacles of capitalist practice at its less acceptable. In Britain we are lucky to have some of the best voluntary bodies, from the Consumers' Association to those which look after our wider civic liberties, especially since government itself can also misbehave and needs to be reined in. The impulse of capitalism is, after all, not unnatural; it is more like a rank flower with a very deep root in human nature, one of the multiple offshoots of self-regard. Regulation of it comes well within J. S. Mill's justifiable definition, in *Liberty*: 'The liberty of the individual must be thus far limited; he must not make himself a nuisance to other people.' This principle should not need heavy promotion; but, here and now, it does need just that.

To sum up

All these processes, then – the widening of *self-choice* as to the desirable style of life and of much else, increased and more widespread *prosperity* coupled with a deep and understandable love of shopping, new *technologies* especially of communication, and an over-arching *capitalist* system, all supported by *class – divisive – feeling* and by the existence of an *under-educated* majority, come together to create the New Society, which J. B. Priestley several decades ago nicely identified as the emerging Admass Society and which it has since become rightly fashionable also to label the Consumer Society or the Commodity Society; a society in love with Things, with Acquisition, with Fashion, with being up-to-date in all kinds of tastes if not in much else, and certainly in little of weight. Not enough for good democratic and civic purposes.

Is all in these introductory pages uniformly depressing? No. I listed at the start clear gains in parts of our lives; above all, the greater freedom to decide the ways we wish to live. My argument has been and will be that, to a degree few of us recognize, those possible gains are being neutralized not so much by political as by commercial forces in whose interest it is that, as individuals, we do not exercise many of the new freedoms. 'The unacceptable face of capitalism' retains much of its smug confidence. Such qualifications belong to the real 'Real World', whose false forms we are constantly invited to accept. It is almost always easier to sing along with the crowd; which is increasingly an international crowd, with the main external influencer the USA; though there for good as well as for ill.

Chapter 2

The View from Above; and a Parade of Persuaders, Defenders and Apologists

'You ask me what it is I do. Well actually,
You know,
I'm partly a liaison man and partly P. R. O.
Essentially I integrate . . .'

('Executive', John Betjeman)

The Parade

The parade has three main cohorts: advertisers, public relations practitioners and sponsorship organizers. The three, especially the first and third, work in various combinations. But, before looking at each in turn, a glance at three other divisions, by height on the pyramid, may be helpful.

At the top are those who sometimes like to be called the 'movers and shakers', though often the title might more fairly be attached to some slightly further down but active and effective each day.

The *Top People* are at the least major shareholders in their business or businesses, members of the boards, not occupiers of daily desks. They may know much about the complex nature of the day-to-day work in producing television or radio programmes or newspapers, or they may have little intrinsic interest in any of those. They do know how to read and interpret accounts, and one or two may have been senior practising accountants them-selves. Or they may be simply, but warily, providers of 'old' or 'new' money, lots of it. They are familiar figures in the City; that is part of their habitual 'contact' life.

Typically, they have a fine house in Kensington or Chelsea or even Westminster, in which they enjoy entertaining the right people (political, commercial or show-biz). They are probably members of Lloyds, the Carlton Club and perhaps the Beefsteak; but not, usually, Groucho's, the Garrick or the Reform. They, or more likely their fathers, may have had a 'good war', preferably in a Guards Regiment. They look and smell as though fresh from the hands of a most expensive hairdresser; they are 'polished' in more than one sense, not hard-faced as are many active execu-tives, but not soft-faced either. At a board meeting most of them will not find it difficult to make tough decisions which protect or advance the price of shares but may bear heavily on colleagues lower down. They pay regular visits to Ascot, Glyndebourne, Henley and the Royal Opera House; they probably regard them-selves as 'very civilized'. They have almost certainly been to one of the 'major' public schools and probably to Oxbridge. They tend to recognize each other not so much by Masonic signals (though that may be possible, as is recognition by school, regi-mental or club neckties) but immediately by stance, accent and gestures.

They have a fairly, but not wholly, modest and certainly comely country house, perhaps in Hampshire, to which they return most weekends, with or without close friends or useful acquaintances. At each of their houses they have a collection of good books, some of them carefully selected first editions, to which they turn from time to time; they eat well, know and enjoy fine wines, and have at least two cars, one expensive and entered on the main firm's accounts, the other a Range Rover or something similar.

Country house interiors can be intriguing; especially if the owner represents 'old' money; then the house may well be entirely un-smart and even a little smelly; as elderly Labradors range floppily from room to room. From North Yorkshire to the heart of Wiltshire, and no doubt further afield, this rule seems to hold quite well.

Their lives, then, are extremely well upholstered and that is the way they themselves look. They take all this as something due to them and their kind; unless they are self-made men who are conscious that they owe it all to nothing external, to no one but themselves. The wives and children of both kinds are as secure as each other in their assumptions about their presents and their futures.

Daddy moves within, and breathes, a different air from all ranks below him and, whilst knowing how to be hail-fellow-well-met with those on lower rungs whom he occasionally meets, he does not dirty his hands with the day-to-day work which brings in dividends as stocks rise. He may be a member of either the Lords or the Commons but, if not in either, knows influential people in both. He or his father were very active indeed in the early fifties when the battle to introduce commercial television was joined, and won; by them. No doubt they were active about the new Communications Bill of 2003.

In one sense such a person belongs to a bygone age; he illustrates the way the British can retain almost unshaken and tolerably unsullied the habits, privileges and guiding assumptions of centuries ago. He and his sort might have been expected to find no place in the modern world of enormous and increasingly global corporations; but his staying power is enormous too; he would not be easily dislodged even if substantial other forces wished to bring that about. If displacement were threatened, he and his type would fight ferociously and, if need be, dirtily; there are no problems and nothing new about that, in peace or war. He has nothing to learn from street anarchists. If a true outsider, say one from the Antipodes, made a 'good offer' for his company, that would not arouse any worryingly historical sentiment in him.

If the good offer were good enough he would urge that it be accepted and himself retire happily to his house in Hampshire. Or he would ensure that his own position on the board was maintained, whatever happened to those below; he is a consummate non-carrier of cans.

Members of the *Second Group* are roughly unified in status or, more accurately, in the estimated importance of their contributions to the organizations' success; but they fall into two bodies quite different in approach and in the work they do.

This group includes, first, the Managing Director or Chief Executive Officer, the day-to-day top desk man. He may well, and with some justice, think of himself as the real 'mover and shaker' in the firm. He is very well paid and has considerable power; the board will not readily go against him except in small matters; disagreements heavier than that may raise the question of resignation – his. He must learn how to 'manage' his board without seeming to do so. He must learn how to make the best use of those in the other half of his group, the 'creatives', to keep on the right side of them, but also to know when to get rid of them if they cease to 'deliver'. He must be able to trust the top men in group three; and again, if that trust fails, to be willing to dismiss them. He is in many respects the lynch pin of the whole organization and his salary and perks reflect that. His importance may be recognized by occasional invitations for the weekend to the chairman of the board's country house. He need not wish for those or, when he goes there, feel like a second-line visitor. He will have his own hinterland of friends and acquaintances, from those who are near his level in similar or quite different professions; he perhaps plays golf and takes expensive foreign holidays well above the Thomson level; his children will go to private and probably public schools though not to those in the thin top layer. He may himself have 'worked his way up' from a state school and not attended university. He does not usually belong to the 'old'-moneyed England and may in spirit have by now half a foot in the USA, having done a Business Management course at one of the pre-eminent universities over there; probably Harvard.

Depending on when he bought it, he may have managed to acquire a house near the centre of London, perhaps in Kensington or Chelsea; if not, he may settle for Notting Hill or even Kennington, or decide to choose from the more expensive desirable suburbs, such as Richmond or Sutton. He may cap these acquisitions with a weekend cottage somewhere in Berkshire. Or he may decide on a single residence forty-odd miles out of London in, say, Farnham, or in one of its charming contiguous villages. Good train service; and a company car will meet him at Waterloo.

The second body in this group is composed of those described earlier as *creatives*; or they could be called the 'ideas people'. In some respects they are, to any organization within the modern mass media, key figures, the stud stallions or germinating bees or silkworms on the industry's mulberry tree. If the appointment of such people proves mistaken, and even if the organization has a competent board, a Chief Executive adept at all aspects of management but with no imaginative sense and no flair for spotting creative ideas and people, then the enterprise is likely to be in trouble. Usually such people need to live under the protection of a good Chief Executive because they are not themselves adept in management ways. Give them good pay and conditions, respect them, and the creative departments are more likely to serve you well, effectively to create, in-house, or to know when and whom to employ from outside, the advertisers, sponsorship fixers, P. R. firms, promoters, who will lift sales or burnish the firm's image, or both. In particular, an effective P. R. department will ensure smooth relations all round but especially with politicians, the press and broadcasting; and will find the right 'celebrities' to be used as promoters of their message.

In almost everything they do, and in this they are not alone in the mass media world, such departments manhandle language to suit their own restrictive but demanding purposes, sometimes with a face-saving romantic edge – as when almost any scheme to promote almost any thing becomes a 'campaign'; nostalgia for a sort of histrionic battle honour will out and produce such inappropriate, such excessive, inflation.

There are almost bound to be tensions between management and the 'creatives'. A version of 'I don't know much about art but I know what I like' haunts many a meeting between management (sometimes with the shadows of management wives in the background) and artists, at which suggested 'campaigns' and 'promotions' are displayed. If the chief 'Creative' director has a good record such interventions become fewer.

Yet what about such discussions as that which produced the much reviled decision by the Post Office: to change its name to 'Consignia'? Since the decision seems almost unbelievable on first sight and after, it would have been instructive and fascinating to be present at the meeting which agreed to the change. The old name had great clarity, was recognized and in a certain sense respected everywhere; it used impeccable English to indicate the organization's central work. There was no justifiable reason to change it except perhaps the itch – which afflicts the mass media in a mass society – to make changes for changes' sake; because it is felt that a 'shake-up' – like a regular personal dose of Andrew's Liver Salts – is always necessary at some point. True, the Post Office was in considerable financial difficulties but only advertising, or P. R. people besotted by the myth of change, and a board in turn unduly influenced by such people, could have accepted change in that area – and to such a name – as being likely to help resolve difficulties.

So the P. R. and advertising men named the usual large fee for their labours; which produced a concocted and confected word with dubious antecedents, chiefly Latin. It belongs nowhere but, in so far as it suggests anything, hints at some vaguely Italian fashion product; an imitation silk scarf sold by mail-order, and advertised at the back of a Sunday colour supplement.

What really happened at that meeting between the external 'creatives' and the Post Office people? Did none of the latter treat the proposal with the scorn it deserves? Did some think that, since they had already spent a lot of money on that particular project, they had better accept the product? Did no one have a sense of good language, for the one suggested is barbaric? How on earth did they, or at least a majority of them, arrive at that foolish proposal; which they were then, or felt for a while, compelled publicly to defend?

A few months after the above lines were written the new chairman of the Post Office announced his own dislike of Consignia' – it sounded like the name of an ageing flamenco dancer – and his decision to drop it. It has since been reported that the reversal will take two years. Which seems a long time. Perhaps some of the delay is due to the phased second repainting of hundreds of vans?

There has recently appeared in the newspapers' financial pages a report on the status of 'Innogy'. Apparently it deals with 'power generation and supply', so one easily sees why it was invented; it suggests 'international energy' most obviously. At a pinch it might also stand for 'International Knowledge' or perhaps that would be better as 'Innology'. Either form is an unhappily ill-rooted invention.

The worst battleground of all, between good sense and the mad world in which money-grubbing takes over as many activities as possible, is probably within commercial television. To a small extent the shadow of the Public Service idea still haunts even some of those in that branch; as they sadly admit now and again. Yet the pressures of the advertisers are unremitting and for them the Public Service idea is as meaningless as ancient lights legislation. They know what they want – the gathering of relevant audiences as much as ever possible – and are not likely to be diverted from that purpose by high-minded talk.

The television companies' boards and managing directors also know on which side their bread is buttered and, though they may pay a little public lip-service to the idea of 'good' broadcasting, to them 'good' almost always has eventually to mean 'popular', which equals large audiences and so equals more profit. Programmes which seem likely to gain relatively small audiences can only be accepted on two grounds: when they are precisely aimed at groups of people who have more than the usual amount of disposable money to spend on more than usually expensive objects; and as an occasional sop to the Public Service principle.

When the routine high-flown or the fake-democratic talk is over, these broadcasters are, see themselves as having to be, in bed with the advertisers. Their staffing (and increasingly that of the BBC) inevitably reflects and so serves those inescapable forces. Since no one can serve two masters, they settle for the more profitable side, and call it 'giving the people what the people want'. If it were otherwise they would become neurotic-ally cross-eyed.

A curious by-way appears here. A small but significant group of budding novelists, some inevitably from Oxbridge, chose to become advertising copywriters as they struggled for recognition (which some have now gained). Copywriting as a suitable prepar-ation or background for serious writing hardly compares with Spinoza's lens-grinding, is more like serving in a massage parlour as a training for marriage. Did they really assume that writing copy would be a good exercise towards the writing of novels? Perhaps in some narrowly technical ways it could. Did they see no conflict of aims between the two kinds of writing; to put the matter simply, one a writing to persuade, the other to explore. The aims of exploratory writing apart, did they see no conflict in their relations to people; people simply as readers, not chiefly as objects to sell to? Apparently not. And did their university education, if they had one, give them no opportunity to consider critically the movements of contemporary society, to question, and in Irving Howe's words, define one essential function of a university: 'to bear witness'? Again, apparently not. The question would presumably seem beside the point to them.

The third group in this topography divides, like the second, into two parts. They are the central, almost hidden, core – the necessary daily workers in the trade. They are divisible into the foremen and the journeymen. The first include the senior production and editorial staff, the senior cameramen, sound operators, electricians, floor managers, sellers of advertising space, newsreaders, and all those in the background whose responsibility it is to see that the complex on-the-ground process works hour after hour, day after day. Many of them, particularly those who have specialist technical skills, take pride in their work. For them, critical choices have been, and continue to be, made higher-up; they are not directly involved in making those choices of aim and purpose, only with their own crafts.

Below them are all the rest, for whose efficient work those immediately above are daily responsible. 'Naturally', these have lower wages, smaller houses and smaller cars than the foremen. With one or two outstanding exceptions, especially among the cameramen, it is unusual to find many in this group who regard their work as a 'profession', or who have a feeling for the value and potential of broadcasting. It is a job, much like any other. That should not be surprising but can still give a slight shock when exhibited publicly. Outstanding exceptions can be found among natural history cameramen, who spend months in jungles or other inhospitable places such as the Arctic, not primarily for the money but for the love of that work.

But who can blame most of the others? Their rewards are not great, they probably recognize the over-riding commercial thrust of those far above them, they have probably not been well-educated outside their particular skills. An assistant soundman may refuse to work a quarter of an hour beyond union-agreed time, even if that causes an extra day of filming a thousand miles from base, and even though it may bring extra pay. He wants to be home for Saturday night and the pub. Those around him would agree to the further day, but he waves the union rulebook at them and they concede. Another will not change an electric light bulb because by union rules that can only be done by a unionized electrician, even though the nearest of those is many miles away. These are two actual examples and to complain about them will of course sound naive to almost all in 'the industry'. They remain rather depressing instances to those who had hoped for a system of broadcasting free from the more restrictive aspects of commercialism and trade unions' reactions to them. They would still exist in a better system – bloody-minded, barrack-room lawyers are always with us – but would then be against the grain, not taken for granted, and their exponents if at all possible not bought off as a matter of routine. Unpleasant defensive practices are inevitable across much capitalist industry and commerce but, given the high origins of British broadcasting, the general loss of its sense of particularly good social purposes is and will remain regrettable

Even those who habitually put in a good day's work are unlikely to have illusions about the drive of the machine they serve. They accommodate, accept the world as it is and expect no more. They probably have families, mortgages and all the rest to maintain. If they become disillusioned, but realize that they are unlikely to find other work which pays as well, they take refuge in two of the principal self-justifications for giving in to what is difficult actually to justify; in that reach-me-down bit of ethical justification: 'If I didn't do it, someone else would . . .'; and in the other favourite crutch; that they: 'have to live in the Real World' – a sentence which is sure to echo through these pages and, being translated, means: 'I must accept the inescapable "reality" of whatever unpleasant shortcuts my present occupation lives by'. 'Real', then, equals 'corrupted'.

A few are case-hardened – cynical – with no regrets. That's the way the world is, always and everywhere, so there is no point at all in 'sticking your neck out'. Maybe what we help to transmit is often trash, but if the bulk of people want that sort of thing that's their look-out, Such unexpectant people do not need even a 'democratic' justification; at a pinch a head-count will do. They know, too, that similar conditions operate in many other industries. Only a tiny minority have ever known (and that is by now at the backs of even their minds) that the arrival of broadcasting in the last century offered the greatest opportunity to create a clear democratic means of communication, one harnessed neither to the profit-making wagon or to political power.

Defenders and Apologists

A recent radio discussion illustrated well one favourite defence by the advertisers. The egregious force of the more extreme advertisements, especially when they are directed at children and even more when Christmas is approaching, had been described by an opponent in a way difficult simply to brush aside. The final defence was then called up: 'Anyway, neither the kids nor the parents are taken in by them. They're too smart for that'. Their opponent, probably because of that inevitable pressure of time, was not able to point out the silly contradictions in that answer: 'You spend millions on those ads. In suitable company you are very proud of them. You even seek prizes at your annual conventions. You *must* believe that you can "take people in". But under attack you disclaim any effect and insist that your intended audiences are rarely deceived. "Sorry – only kidding."' The lies in the ads themselves are compounded by a lie in their defence.

No doubt many parents see through the ads and some of those may resist their children's nagging and point out the tricks. To say that many other people are not so sophisticated is predictably to be accused of being 'undemocratic', of under-estimating 'the common man'. Most politicians and a good many journalists respond in that way; that unwillingness goes with their professions. Unpalatable or not, this unhappy fact about 'the common man' should be recognized more often. Given the low level of literacy of many people, the claim that many are persuaded by these advertisements and so, it follows, are their children, is obviously well-founded. If we faced it, we could do more to reduce its force.

A favourite, fairly recent, device, one which meets criticism half-way, is meant to work by exaggerating the qualities for which many advertisements are criticized. The old sequences for after-dinner mints were meant to suggest that the best hostesses served them. They offered a world above that of the majority of their audiences; that, say, of a novelette, rather plush middle-class. Something to aspire to, if only intermittently, especially by the lower middle-class. That kind of 'campaign' became stale and unconvincing. So let us now, some obviously decided, blow it up into cartoon-like proportions and show chocolates being handed round at a diplomatic reception and received with exclamations of rapture. Not many, one might hope, would take that at face value. More would see it as a confident exaggeration carried through amusingly by deliberate ham-acting – 'only kidding', again. From it, the 'creative' mind behind might expect its caricature to be enjoyed and its viewers to be tickled and so not to be at the least ill-disposed towards those chocolates. Less sophisticated viewers might be tempted to provide those chocolates to guests, having been affected by the exaggerated glamour, and taken it straight.

Less obvious – cleverer – very much a further stage ahead in their approach, are those advertisements which do not play off against class-aspirations but are plainly amusing or even shocking, which simply tickle our funny-bones. 'Laugh and the world laughs with you.' The product being advertised may be only obliquely mentioned and sometimes hardly that but, it is clearly hoped, a feeling of mild even surreal and eye-catching fun or surprise (for example, Zurich Insurance Company's flying pigs) will have been created towards it. Advertising does indeed attract very many highly 'creative' minds. 'Eye-catching' recalls some fairly recent Benetton efforts, in which the product being supposedly advertised is scarcely even tangential to the pictures.

One could continue for page after page about the character of early twenty-first century advertising; some publications already do so. Here, our concern is with advertising's likely effects, and especially with those advertisements which work by playing on ignorance, lack of education or childhood innocence. It would be easy to point to whole ranges of advertisements which even today work by excessive exaggeration meant to be taken literally – about the astounding qualities of facial creams, the astonishing speed of some motorcars, the remarkable power of some beers to make the drinker attractive (especially to willing young women), the beauty of almost unbelievably cheap furniture and fitted kitchens, the wonderfully friendly offers of loans, and so on and on. Very many of us are still duped and not only those in the lower social groups. It is important to recognize this, to take this at least directly, and not to shrug it off with a knowing smile. One of the worst features on some satellite channels are the repetitive and insistent hard-sells by finance houses willing to pay off your debts and compound them into one sum you then owe to them. They are obviously addressed to the relatively innocent and, I should have thought, need the attention of the Advertising Standards Authority. I have seen the results of such offers at first hand, enough to wish them banned. 'There's no such thing as a free lunch' should be known in the lower reaches of society.

One can at least take some comfort in the fact that most advertisements can now be subject to objective scrutiny: by, among others, the Consumer's Association, the BBC's 'Watchdog' and similar programmes, and the *Guardian*'s 'Dear Anna' page. The obvious limitations in all those is that they tend to be joined, watched or read almost entirely by those who are already alert to the problems; in this, they are like most of the food programmes which are clearly aimed at what one might call the upper-lower middle-class (and those who seek to be like them) and above. In both areas more programmes specifically aimed below that level could be useful. They would have to compete, though, with those programmes, by now the majority (not simply advertisements), designed to keep viewers hooked and satisfied, particularly unwilling to turn to anything which looks 'improving'; a severe challenge to Public Service-minded producers, but a good one. In all these things, those lacking in much education are most affected and most relentlessly targeted. The admen have here to get round what remains – and in some people and places it does remain – of the old working-class ability to recognize and 'take the mickey' out of the confidence-tricksters. As we have seen, the cleverer 'creative minds' can even engage that 'no flies on Charlie' spirit to their own ends. We will have to raise this point from different angles again and again: we are a society divided by both class and education, with large groups more gullible than they should be if they are to survive successfully in today's world.

Public Relations people are threatened by no such objective tests. They have no objectively testable products. They deal only in words, words for rootless opinions – opinions not connected to the movement of logic or true feeling. Words can be very powerful indeed; it is much more difficult to assess them than to judge that a much-hyped settee, splendid looking on television, will prove after a few months use to be cheaply put together. The language of advertisements has proved to be, in a good modern phrase, 'all smoke and mirrors'; or in an older expression: 'all wind and water', or even: 'all wind and piss'.

Yes, there are some – a very few – P. R. and advertising organizations which claim ethical standards; and a few do live up to that claim; the rest neither claim nor exhibit such standards. The law can to some degree restrict them, but their liberty is great, more than enough for their scrubby purposes. The relation to 'truth' in their writing is tenuous, a side issue. If a disinterested writer (W) aims first to get down the truth of what he or she has to say about the subject (S) being written about, and hopes by that to reach, on the far side, an unknown reader (R) – the movement being W to S to R – then the position of the P. R. writer is different, and in a way more tortuous. There is no straight line from writer through subject to reader. There is a line from writer to subject (the ideas or opinions or goods being promoted), or more accurately to those elements in the subject which seem most likely to capture the reader; then back for the finding of words for those elements, back again to who is paying for the ads, and so out to the reader with that cleverly edited material. This is writing for, so far as possible, a pre-determined effect on the reader (no doubt many highly successful writers, especially of popular fiction, have similar aims). The writer of P. R. prose shares with many a popularity seeking writer of fiction the wish as early as possible to hook readers and keep them hooked. This is not the same as hoping to engross the reader by truth of observation and insight. The writer of popular fiction hopes to engage the reader so that each book and its successors are read; that is a fairly direct transaction. The P. R. writer aims to bring the reader to someone else's point of view so as to further that someone's ends with a vote or a purchase. This is verbal persuasion as propaganda in its pure, dictionary sense. The writer wishes to incline you to see the world – or a certain part of the world – as it is there offered on behalf of a third party, who wishes to have your good opinion but cannot himself ensure that result as well as can a hired somebody who has 'a way with words'. Any search for a sort of 'truth' yields to the promotion of specific angles for the sake of the paymaster. P. R. writers deal with words, but abuse them; they are the fallen – gone to the dogs – cousins of honest writers.

It is therefore in tones of voice that the advertising writer and the P. R. executive most often come together. Those tones run a long gamut from the hectoring or frightening hard-sell right through to the confidentially cooing and flattering, passing on the way the blokey countryman, the silkily confiding neighbour, the phony-serious scientist and dozens of others. The commitment to observed and respected truth is the first casualty of the P. R. trade. Its practitioners are the 'diplomats' of the Mass Media world ('sent to lie, at home and abroad, for the sake of their employers').

Public Relations firms are aware of the suspicion in which they are held by most of those who have thought at all about their practices; surprisingly few have. Those who have looked in the public mirror attempt to salve their consciences or at the least to assuage the critics by exercising a certain amount of what they call 'pro bono' work, done without charge for the good of the community, *pro bono publico*. If the area chosen for such work involves questions of well-founded cultural judgment, the limitations of their thinking are soon apparent.

One such firm agreed to undertake pro bono work for a charity concerned with promoting *good* reading, especially by children. A tricky field, that, requiring some literary understanding and some understanding of the pressures on authors who want to 'see life straight and see it whole'. When the firm's beautifully presented report was ready the writer, a fairly junior man, was accompanied by one more senior; smooth, well-dressed, elegant, with unshaken confidence.

He soon confidently revealed that, insofar as he had thought at all about writing and books, his vision was entirely constrained by the market and marketing promotions, by the cult of the best-seller. He implied that the members of the charity were out of touch and so had a fuddy-duddy idea of how to promote the sales (not so much the reading) of books; he told them they should learn from the marketing of the Booker Prize; that brought books to attention in all the main media and so the winners sold well. Himself, he didn't have much time to read during the normal working week, or even year, but his wife packed each year's Booker short-listed novels for their annual holiday. Thus even he, an enormously preoccupied executive, was yearly made aware of the world of good books. His thoughts on the subject were entirely contained within the Mass Communications Circle and Cycle (Bestsellers Branch).

Within those terms what he said made its own kind of sense; but it had no useful relation to the aims of the charity. He was received in polite silence; after all, he and his junior had given their services without charge. The members of the charity could have pointed out that Booker novels needed no further promotion from them; the system ensured that. As to novels, the charity was concerned to promote (especially for children) not the latest of bestsellers for all ages, which were already heavily promoted by publishers, booksellers and, oddly enough, by some public libraries. Their concern was with bringing to the attention of many more people, to think now only of writers of the last two centuries: Austen, Dickens, Trollope, Hardy, James, Conrad, Forster, Lawrence, Greene and others. Writers such as those have contributed to the Art of the Novel, to what Lawrence happily considered the one bright book of life.

Sponsorship

More will need to be said about sponsorship when celebrities are considered. The first point to be made here is that the practice by now covers activities far wider than the uses – misuses – of those who happen at any particular moment to be greatly in the public eye. Supermarkets scatter sponsorship like multi-coloured and multi-sized confetti: relatively small sums to local good causes, schools, old people's homes and the like; and so on to national affairs: musical competitions, sports, arts buildings and so forth. It is as hard to resist such things as it is to resist dona-tions from the National Lottery. Some of the Great and Good see no problem here. The late Lord Goodman was ready to say, in his best orotund manner: 'Sir, I would take money from the Devil himself if it helped the arts to flourish.' One can see the point, whilst remembering the old warning about long spoons.

So, even if the money is taken with no hint of a feeling of guilt, those coins should be bitten twice and no self-serving conditions on which the giver might like to insist should be accepted if they run against the receiver's better judgement. Many of those are so glad, relieved, to have the money that they hesitate to ask any possibly inhibiting questions. Questioned themselves, most really do not see any problem; or purport not to. It is when one turns the microscope even more closely that difficulties begin to show, as in donations to schools, many of which are now very short indeed of disposable funds. Some have enlisted their pupils and their pupils' families to save coupons towards the acquisition of computers from their local supermarket. That restricts the parents' choice of places at which to shop (which is part of the point); and one needs literally thousands of coupons before a computer comes into view.

Worse is the agreement made by some schools, for a 'con-sideration', to advise (or at least half-insist) that school uniforms be bought only at a designated shop in town. Did it not occur to the consenting Heads that they were restricting the parents' choice and freedom to find the best bargain, that which fitted their perhaps thin purses?

Worst of all is the practice in some schools of allowing, for a payment of rent, fast food and drinks manufacturers to put their machines in the corridors. That has been slightly looked at earlier. One can add here that their presence will encourage the pupils and some of their parents to think that there is no problem about the amount of such drinks consumed; that they have the schools' approval. Any Head who replies that, given its shortage of disposable funds, the school had little choice in the matter should, in a good old-fashioned phrase: 'Have his – or her – head read.' As we have seen, some Heads join the ranks not exactly of the defenders and apologists already described; they do join the ranks of the soft-centred inadvertent apologists. So does any local education authority which chooses to ignore the practice or justifies it on libertarian grounds; and the Department of Education and Skills, which also leaves the decision to Heads. All of them are probably ready to wheel out one of the usual dismissals, of 'straight-laced' or 'po-faced puritans' or their kind. As on so many subjects discussed in these pages, the level of public debate is unjustifiably low, and takes refuge in throwing around escapist sound-bites, old and new, instead of trying to come to terms with pressing social and individual changes and the questions, cheering or depressing, which they raise.

Particularly lax are some highly educated people – people who 'should know better'. Some enjoy exercising a mild *nostalgie de la boue* by watching television programmes which they admit are 'cretinous' just to show they are not precious, not out-of-touch highbrows, just ordinary chaps; and they do enjoy them. Indeed, some programmes on television can fascinate with their revelations, often melodramatic, of 'how the other half lives', and in particular of how so very many are willing to make fools of themselves if that will get them on to the 'box'. Most television slummers have never looked at the questions raised by such programmes, perhaps again being afraid to be thought 'spoil sports' – a phrase actually used by a cabinet minister on hearing a constituent's reservations about the National Lottery programmes.

Slightly off our main theme but typical of this lack, or refusal, is the acceptance of Classic FM by some who might be expected to be dismissive of truncated classical music. One can for an odd half-hour or so enjoy listening to that station. Soon doubts creep in. It lives by playing most of the time and especially during the day, morsels of whole works, the more attractive morsels, the generally favoured movement of a symphony or concerto, or the whole of some shorter piece known to be extremely popular; say, Vivaldi's *Four Seasons*. Cherry-picking; like isolating the smile of the Mona Lisa on a postcard; or perhaps focusing only on the nether parts of Michael Angelo's 'David'. By now they are totally assured, having used market research to identify just which few hundred or so bits their audience most likes. One can imagine the chagrin of a composer who has toiled over the complex structure of a piece, on hearing again and again a 'choice' bit pulled out for a few minutes playing, before the move to another composer's similarly bleeding chunk. Not much 'onward and upward' there.

Rather, it recalls Hannah More's lines on similar literary operators: '. . . those literary cooks/Who skim the cream off others' books/And ruin half an author's graces/By plucking *bon mots* from their places'.

Plainly those who run such a programme know what they are doing. They want as large and constant an audience as possible; they know that that central audience is already acquainted, more or less, with 'the best bits' of classical music. It is not their purpose to encourage a moving-out, to suggest that making the effort to stay with a composition may bring unexpected enjoyment. Too many listeners would be lost to the station whilst that was going on; better to offer a constant diet of savoury cocktail snacks. We are back again with yet another version of the carousel – on which more and more people are invited to stay as it goes constantly round and round – as against the escalator, by ascending which one could, in out-of-date language, gain fuller and better pleasures. This contrast is, as we have seen and will see again, one of the cardinal identifying features of the mass society.

'[Don't] allow them to inject you with Glamour, Sport, Sensational News, and all the other De Luxe nonsense. As if they were filling you with anaesthetic.' J. B. Priestley's *Letter to a Returning*

Serviceman is as usual forthright and also prescient; almost sixty years on it is as relevant as when it was written.

It is justifiably pugnacious about those who service the process, including the defenders and apologists; which raises the question of what really are their unspoken – we know what their public protestations are – attitudes to their audiences. It has to be said straightaway that some, probably most, see no ethical problem at all arising from their work; they 'believe in' their product and see nothing wrong in trumpeting its virtues; they do not ask many questions about the language the copywriters use to do that; they are substantially at ease with themselves, and may even do some voluntary social work or give money to several charities, as well as loving their children and taking the dog for walks. They probably believe they are being democratic, in refusing to judge any habits – other than the plainly criminal – of their fellow citizens. We saw earlier that that attitude can extend right to the top of the public or academic tree. It can only survive easily if those who hold it ignore powerful forces outside their 'fellow citizens' which bear heavily on them all but especially on the under-educated and so do damage, precisely, to an emerging democracy.

At the far end of this range of people within the persuading media are, yet again, the unabashedly cynical, those who believe that 'it's their lookout' if they fall for whatever is cooked up for them. In between are those who are not high-minded about the merits of their product, but think it's probably no better nor worse than others in the field, but who are not cynical – at least not openly. These are among the most interesting, the ones who live with a barely disguised contempt for the methods they use and, even more deeply disguised, for those they seek to reach. Perhaps the most interesting of all in this company are those in whom the contempt is disguised even from themselves and who, if that suggestion is put to them, react with genuine anger. 'These deeds must not be thought / After these ways; so, it will make us mad.'

People of that kind, particularly, make use of one of the defender's favourite rejoinders: that they truly reflect the character of their audiences, or they would not succeed. 'We speak to and for the Common Man; we are his voice,' as one editor of a popular newspaper put it. There is some truth in that. If the world they present were alien to their audiences they would soon be without audiences. They must speak to some attitudes, some hopes and fears, some prejudices, some enthusiasms and some limitations. But only some at any given time, and others at no time; there must be selection. There is, to take an extreme example, little or no room in this world for any intellectual or imaginative interests – for, say, poets – except in the occasional advert which produces a stereotype and makes fun of it. There is much room for things romantic; for the English love of patent medicines (which Graham Greene took note of, as he did with much popular song of the thirties: 'The world's wet mouth lamenting over life'); for the obsession with football, but not so much for other sports since some are still so class-divided. Television has opened this area, to some extent; snooker, if that is listed as a sport, is a striking example, especially in view of its roots. These operators almost entirely ignore the arts; their 'mind-set', or that projected on to their audience is thoroughly low level, and confident in being so; it is selective in a way which makes Classic FM seem posh; or vaguely inclined that way.

They ignore whole ranges of, let us say, working-class life or present it only in caricature; as with neighbourliness or, at the other extreme, narrow xenophobia. So they miss much (and though much remains) in general they know what buttons they need to press, buttons which are true to some common attitudes, not the whole truth but enough to allow the claim that these voices do speak for, reflect, 'ordinary folk'. 'Giving the people what the people want' is not a simple process; it requires an ear and eye able to detect those attitudes which are true to people, but not the whole truth, and which serve the needs of the writer or the writer's employer's purposes. When those things come together there is successful communication – partial, but it can seem the whole.

Many of today's 'professions' award themselves that title without justification. Their language rules them out and cannot be purified by any business school. A 'profession' has its own form of the Hippocratic Oath, which expresses the human values its members obey, e.g. curing the sick. They do not have ulterior purposes. An 'awful' – in two senses – image surfaces again: of expensively dressed or 'power-dressed' adults sitting round a table plotting, conspiring and seeking to persuade tens of thousands of housewives to buy the new washing powder and so enter a new world. It can be found comical. Or criticism can be unconvincingly brushed aside as futile, ineffective on the grounds that people are much too knowing to be taken in. But it raises the thought that such 'authors' would be better employed in the local councils' cleaning departments; in their spare time, perhaps, trying to write honestly about something; anything.

Chapter 3

From Consumption, Concentration, Classless Compartments to Relativism

'Assume particular stages of development in production, commerce and consumption and you will have a corresponding social constitution, a corresponding organization of the family, of orders and of classes . . .'

(Karl Marx, 'Letter to P. V. Annenkov', 26 December 1846)

Tools of the Trade

Among the main characteristics of mass society, and of its loyal servants the mass media are, then, the movements towards levelling which brings the addiction to head-counting, and to the false democracy of populism. These are encouraged by, and in turn serve, the buying-and-shopping society – the society of consumerism as more and more goods and more and more opinions, from burgers to politics, can be produced for more and more people to swallow, people who are thereby more and more seen as masses. Everything seems to be for sale, so everything has its price. All this within the West or developed world, of course. 'Distracted by distraction from distraction.'

Hence concentration which, as if paradoxically, encourages the thin reductionism of things and ideas – reduction to a condition of more and more easily-swallowed pap. The bedrock of all

47

these forces and emergings is, has to be, relativism, the condition in which nothing really matters except those things which can be consumed without there ever arising the question of whether some are better than others. They must all be 'all right' because millions consume them; mass consumption implies mass approval. 'Whatever is, is right', so long as it has been validated by mass acceptance. That is all you know and all you need to know; for the moment and of the moment. Since so many things are quickly and easily produced, they must be placed on a never-ending conveyor belt constantly fed at the front but with its material just as constantly dropping into nothingness at the end. If not, then the machines will have to stop. All, as in each week's music chart, this season's fashions in dress, this December's books of the year.

Deviations are dangerous; they disperse. You are instantly forgiven if you know little more than names from this season's fashions or views. BBC Radio 4 put out a trailer for a programme by or about Octavio Paz. The announcer added, perhaps on his own initiative, to be ballsy: 'And if you haven't heard of him, whose fault is that; yours or his?' Brash ignorance flaunting its assumed fellowship with crowds of others.

This society talks all the time; it can never 'let people be'; 'presentation' is all; it must constantly aim at that point which is the place where millions come together. 'The World's 100 Best Films' as discovered by a totally unselective poll, in which most respondents are likely to have seen only a fraction of the entries, and even fewer have actually thought before being invited to put their judgements in order. 'The 100 Films Most Easily Dredged from Memory in a Straw Poll' would be a more accurate title; or simply 'A Rough Trawl to Discover the 100 most *Popular* Films'.

There are cracks in the fabric: one of the many polls for the best this or that had a fit of honesty and did indeed change its name to the 'The Most Popular . . .'. There is an intriguing contradiction here: such polls are plainly levelling since they imply that any one person's judgement is as good as anyone else's, but they go on to put the one hundred or so in order; so *one* must be thought the best. But no – no entry has been the result of a vote for the very *best*. The so-called 'best' is that one out of the hundred which is most often named. Levelling with ordering by repetition, but not judging; at bottom, valueless.

So, since between individuals there can now be no deference, no looking up, or sense of superiority in looking down, this has also to be the world of immediate friendships, where the instant use of first names suggests near but brief intimacy. Only the surly, the taciturn or the brave will reject this false bonhomie. There can in the same context be strange lapses from what might be thought minimum courtesy towards one who is, in a hardly permitted word in this concourse of pals, 'a stranger'. Conversely, the presenters of the 'Today' programme on the BBC's Radio 4 do not adopt first names but almost always fail to say 'Good Morning' before they begin to question a new interviewee. The brave or sticklers for 'old-fashioned courtesy' will themselves interrupt the first question with their own formally stressed opening: 'Good Morning'. Some of the presenters make an exception for particularly distinguished interviewees; the finely honed British sense of deference is likely to come into play then, with even the most pugnacious of questioners.

Few will stand out against the insistent half-hidden appeal to common taste not always because they are afraid but sometimes because they do not wish to appear impolite by going against the tide which is apparently carrying with it so many millions of 'ordinary decent folk'. A bolder kindness would be to speak out and say that rubbish is rubbish – as occurred with a press conference to announce the short-list for a recent annual Booker Award. One journalist asked why a certain novel did not appear on that list since it had been praised, and suggested as the proper winner, by so many of his and other newspapers' readers. A member of the judging committee answered with unusual directness, to the effect that the prize was for the best novel in literary terms, not the most popular. One wondered whether that journalist realized that a new intellectual panorama was being opened before him.

Incidentally, that phrase 'in literary terms' recalls another, less intelligent, use of the word 'literary' in this area. Many thousands of novels are published each year whose aim is chiefly to become bestsellers; most have little to recommend them, even some of those which succeed in their aim. Within the whole number are a few for which it is not easy to find a due epithet. They have been written with the subject rather than a possible readership precisely in mind; they are 'serious' in that they try to explore their subject honestly and to capture it and its settings in the right words. It wouldn't do for a reviewer to call them 'serious' novels, for that might imply that the rest were 'unserious', 'light' or even 'negligible'. 'Quality novel' would be even more insulting to all the rest ('a quality novel for quality time'); and 'upmarket' would take us into exactly what we are trying to leave – the market and its divisions. So we divide the species into two; on the one hand the 'novel' itself with no epithet, usually not even 'the popular novel' since even that might seem slightly lowering. So: 'the novel' on the one hand, in the centre of attention; and on the other 'the literary novel' which indicates, one supposes, the sort of novel which only literary people read and we all know that they are a snobbish breed. Whoever invented that division did well by his trade, and badly for the understanding of the achievements of the novel.

This 'democratic' attitude can produce a sort of totalitarianism of its own, a collective and inevitably lowbrow world in which all are expected to toe the line, to go the way that world is going. To modify Dr Johnson's words, we are pressed: 'To rejoice at concurring with the opinions held up to and for the common man' simply to take them as given, unassailable. This is a hidden censorship of considerable force.

50

It is not an accidental process but arises from that insistent urge, on those who make goods or push ideas, to concentrate the market and opinions. Concentration becomes confinement, but the atmosphere of the time does not encourage one to realize that. It must insist that all are equal – at the check-out and increasingly before that other characteristic feature, the 'brand names' (there have now emerged 'brand opinions'). All are equal in the almost unseen loss of freedom which follows.

So again the claim that this approach is an instance of democracy at work is a lie. True democracy allows each person or as many as wish it to be individuals – quirky, rough at the edges, salty not saccharine. The self-righteous assurance of populism, that it knows what people want and how to give it to them is based on a narrowing and distortion of vision. To those who would a few decades ago have undoubtedly belonged to the working-class and who were daily, at work and at play, reminded of that, this pomegranate can seem attractive. 'Freedom; we're as good as anyone else now.' But it is a delusion; they are now caught in a new and almost all-encompassing net, not now for the benefit of 'those above us' but for those all-levelling false friends (some of whom will be drawn from their own ranks). Dismantling the snobberies of social class is fine; to fall then into the explicit rejection of any difference of worth whilst at the same time encouraging a new range of differences and snobberies, based on the contrasts between a populist mass and a meritocratic minority; this is a very bad bargain.

Such a society has to have a great range of cooing calls, invitations to belong to the great congregation of the majority. This is above all intrinsic to the entirely and naturally loose practice of television; for television 'personalities' and those who promote them know that potentially their audiences may indeed be 'classless'; or, more accurately, mixed multi-class. They cannot endure divisive speech, utterances which suggest that the majority may be mistaken, that a minority may be more in the truth.

Some years ago I was interviewed by a major television person-ality about what had begun to be called the Paperback Revolution, the huge rise in paperback sales. Didn't this indicate a large and probably permanent improvement in taste, I was asked. I answered that that was not likely since the great bulk of the paperbacks were of no value (perhaps I should have said 'no literary value'), being sex and violence, gangster, or romantic and entirely escapist novels and the like. There were also some novels of quality, especially from the nineteenth century, since that avoided copyright. Those were often out of print, so that was a gain; they were found a place because the machines for the pulp paperbacks had spare capacity; they were hitching a ride, cheaply. The interviewer turned to camera and said to his unseen millions: 'Well, that puts us in our place, doesn't it?' He was serious, set back, not simply uttering what he believed to be his viewers' reactions. I was 'badly out of line', so he made a bold appeal to the not-to-be-challenged rightness of the average viewers as he imagined them. This Shakespearian 'cry to call fools into a circle' was a conclusive indication that that man was worth every penny of his very large contract.

More recently, again in a television interview, an interviewee uttered an unconventional and unpopular opinion: 'No, I do not think that Pavarotti in the Park will greatly add to the audience for classical music.' The interviewer responded with one of the stock formulations of his kind: 'But surely you are not saying . . .' in a tone laced with near-outrage that someone had stepped so perversely out of the communal warm bath. Those two instances embody two truisms of mass society: that the mass of people cannot be mistaken, whatever they continue to accept, and that they should remain happily on what I have called the carousel – no hint of any 'onward and upward' progress in taste, from Pavarotti's selected aria to the whole of *Turandot*, only an end-lessly level and circular ride which television itself does much to promote.

Personalities such as the two cited above are the templates of received taste; with their own self-saving vocabulary; they like to think of themselves as hospitable and Catholic, both, in this, case synonyms for minds 'so wide-open that they can't close on anything solid' and non-judgemental. They may, though, in time, accept indisputable greatness that doesn't threaten from a safe distance. But if Shakespeare or Dickens were writing today it would not be safe to bank on the recognition of their quality from recent, loudly and insistently presented, bestsellers or even from heavily promoted, would-be-highbrow, novels. Similarly, it would be simply assumed that the lyrics of the latest number one pop song were not to be reduced by comparison with those of Mahler, if he were of their generation. They would be likely to claim that such distinctions were merely inventions of artistic snobs; or to seize on another favourite placebo, which will be looked at later: 'they're good for their kind'. Another favoured assertion is that if Dickens, say, were alive today he would be writing long-running television soap operas; with Shakespeare no doubt invited to offer eight-part Edwardian dramas; the offers would, naturally, be accepted. To do otherwise would be unthinkable.

Decline of the News

Examples of these continuous and all-invading movements abound. Latterly, they have been especially encroaching on the presentation of television news. The news has been one of the latest features to have the definition of its public service remit challenged. This is particularly regrettable since in many respects it has been – as it should be – the natural home for the realization of some major public service principles; notably the aim to be, so far as possible, objective and to have a well-thought through approach to priorities. Even now, much in the practice of broadcast news embraces many of those principles. As compared with much of the popular press, it is usually true to many of those guiding lights. Most broadcasting journalists have retained a fairly confident sense of knowing what 'news' in Britain should be, its due order in any bulletin, its proper length and style of treatment; in short, of relative degrees of importance.

It is hampered by regularity of form and frequency, by the assumption that at six o'clock each evening, there will be at least enough 'news' to fill each slot and that that will also offer something which can be called 'the main news'. Life is not like that, of course; some days there is little that can properly be called 'news'. But who imagines that one day the newscaster will say: 'There is no news today'? There has to be, enough to fill the spaces allotted to it; it is that kind of commodity.

The editors of news are not alone. Their sense of what is news has been culturally conditioned as to what is included, where and how. They are, in the jargon, structuring reality. That structure will be determined by the often unexamined, largely subcutaneous 'spirit of the time', which itself is defined by the current engines of persuasion. Obviously, it has had, by legislation, to steer clear of the vulgar and obscene; it assumes that it has, even now, to give more time and a greater priority to Royal doings than some professionals would think necessary and which foreigners find odd in a twenty-first-century 'democracy'; it gives great – perhaps undue – prominence to sport, with special but by no means slavish regard to their class affiliations, from football to horse-racing. It has done much to reduce the class-connections of some sports.

Always at the back of most serious journalists' minds there has been a sense of meaningful structures: that political news – home and abroad – matters and, unless it is slight or very far away indeed, deserves a high ranking. These are among the 'oughts' and 'shoulds' of the trade. That many people find some parts of the national news bulletins boring and wait for the more gossipy items, or those who feel that sport should not be given the time it is. It is, rather, a challenge to present news items understandably without denaturing meaning – to get across without selling out.

Traditional assumptions about priorities are now being increasingly challenged. One senior executive in commercial television has already publicly announced his view that the priorities of place and duration of news bulletins presentation should by decided by 'the viewers' own sense of such things; so bulletins should be 'lightened' (which in that context means 'made shallower and narrower'). The background motto is, of course: 'If that is what most viewers want, it would be undemocratic of us not to give it to them.' Which would mean that sport would be placed even higher, probably by a further overestimation of its appeal as compared with that of other subjects; and political news lower; in between would be a number of 'ooh-ah' items, on the lines exemplified by the more popular Sunday newspapers. 'Ooh-ah' appeal has been defined as a mixture of fear, cruelty and collective self-righteousness. There is no sense of a duty to imply: 'Look, this is important for all of us and deserves attention early.'

Certainly, every effort can and should be made to ensure that that presentation is accessible; but not, as in so much, falsely 'democratic'; not at the cost of lowering it with gimmicks thought to make 'heavy' news more palatable, without much thought as to whether in the process the facts of the news and comment upon it are presented in so reductive a way as to damage the necessary impact of important items.

That movement is already well under way, especially when sport is concerned. In the autumn of 2001, professional footballers threatened to strike. This was discussed at length on television news, as the first item. The very much more important news from Afghanistan on that day, the fall of Mazar-i-Sharif, came later. Similarly, on another day the death of a famous football manager led the evening news; at the time the fighting

in Serbia was intensifying. The famous manager appeared again
at the end of the news: 'The main news tonight is . . .' At that
point one wondered what proportion of the population would
think that that death really was the main news of the day; perhaps
a majority? Even so, I think that a professional misjudgement.
Much the same pattern was repeated when the athlete Linford
Christie was, by the British authorities at least, cleared of drug
charges. And what bizarre pattern of news values led both the
BBC and commercial television to lead the main evening bulletin
with news of Paula Yates' death?

All this contrasts with the broader and more balanced selection of news on Channel 4; and now, even more, with the news
on BBC4. That has both horizontality (a wide geographic and
subject range) and verticality (proper depths of treatment). It
knows its audience is very small and that to seek to widen it substantially would be to join in competition with the large analogue
channels; on their terms.

To return to football; obviously, the traditional interest in 'the
beautiful game' has been increased if not enhanced recently by
its rampant commercialization, from the vast transfer fees and
the vast salaries paid to the most successful players, through to
the sale of club shirts, shorts and all the other memorabilia. The
football authorities have responded rapaciously to the developing compound of idolatry with levelling, Typically, a linguistic
device supports the levelling impulse; the top division is the
Premier; the one below is the First; no one seems to mind the
near tautology.

Levelling in the news is, by now, advanced. When the severe
new cuts in North Sea fishing were proposed by Brussels most
main television news gave much space to moving interviews with
fishermen at their harbours. Nothing was then said about the scientific case for the cuts, about whether they were well-founded;
and, if so, whether they were necessary to protect the growth of
fish stocks for the next generation of fishermen. The fishermen

who were chosen to speak all wanted simply to go on fishing as usual. Those items were one-sided, heart-string pullers.

Did the editors of the varied bulletins described above share the underlying pattern of values? If so, the unpleasant change is already far advanced. Or did they say to themselves and others: 'This'll bring them in'? Is there a high level of cynicism in those offices? Perhaps the second attitude is preferable to the first. To discover that editors of national television news did share that shallow idea of orders of importance would be depressing. Perhaps some are easy in having a twin-compartment mind; one for their native intelligence, the other for the job and what they think the audience thinks. At least, cynicism can be a sort of judgement, an unspoken but unenforced rejection.

One begins to wonder how those broadcasting journalists are selected, and whether they are given any training or whether they are left to the comforting myth that 'training on the job' is always best. It also transmits bad, socially and psychologically ignorant habits from generation to generation; with confidence. Is the explanation of the public service idea, within BBC training at least, given any time at all? In the impressive days when Oliver Whitley was Head of the Personnel Department, staff were given introductions to British culture and its relations to the public service idea. But that was long ago.

It would be wrong to suggest that these habits are to be found only in broadcasting; they are obvious in much of the press. Those two media are the outstanding examples of levelling, the masters of the mass audiences. But levelling grows and spreads everywhere; to publishing, for example. The cult of the bestseller and its effect on the publishing of more exploratory (serious, original, non-conventional, not predictable) works increases.

Just one example – an editor at a publisher of the Holy Bible justifies a change, a reduction, in the title: 'It's just called the Bible now. We dropped the word Holy to give it more mass-market appeal.' Which 'mass market'? Of Muslims, agnostics, atheists or humanists? Or the audiences for paperback romances? It is very hard to understand just who he sees as the new audience; unless he believes there are many readers out there who would buy the Bible so long as it does not purport to be Holy Writ. Perhaps they should be offered the King James' version; that at least has 'literary merit'. No, that would put off any 'mass market'. But it would be hard to improve on that spokesman's statement of aims above – as a justification for neglecting the values of the uncertain few so as to coax the assured many. Whether the statement has any basis in the reality of possible audiences is another and dubious matter.

From those new angles, public interest must always yield to human interest; which must be exploited because it is rightly believed that that will predictably 'deliver', in television as in the popular press, the largest solid block of audiences. From that belief and the constant pressures it induces there emerges, especially in the tabloid press, a number of unattractive phenomena: the paparazzi, the door-stoppers, the deceptive interviewers and all other invaders of privacy; side by side with diatribes especially addressed to 'social security scroungers', the Social Services, and immigrants in general. Perhaps we should be marginally grateful that their worst coarsenesses are occasionally partnered by purported warm-heartedness?

Not really; the warm hearts are usually merely soppy so the coarseness wins in the end. Jingoism, intellectual narrow-mindedness, boorish emotional self-indulgence, twinned with soft-focus sentimentality about children, pets, members of the Royal family and television personalities (though if the latter misbehave, especially sexually, they are subjected for a time to the finger-wagging mode); this mixture does not make up a balanced and intelligent combination for news or current affairs. There used to be a dismissive phrase, popular among working-class people, for those who exhibited a committed sense of what was required by their own rotten jobs: 'Oh, they're any way for a rotten apple.' That serves well for the process by which human interest is reduced to slight items which may entertain.

Catch-penny popularization of the news and related programmes is, then, already underway in much of broadcasting, especially on television, and in the BBC as in the commercial channels. Only the few already named, notably Channel 4 (see later), BBC4 (also see later) and Radio 4, are to some degree not going down that path at present, or, perhaps, 'for the present'. As we have seen, other journalists are already changing the agenda and making themselves feel righteous about it.

There is a further bonding in this search for 'mass human interest'. We are spoken to as members of a homogeneous majority all going in the same direction; but have to be made to feel, at the same time (though this is a rather difficult trick), that we are being addressed as individuals, single and separate 'you's'. If that is too difficult, we are offered a sort of emotional twinning, in which we become 'individuals making choices within the mass media', are not simply carried along by them as are other people. As in advertisements for those industrialized foods which are attractively packaged and described as if addressed to a proudly discriminating individual: 'You and X . . . will have a great name for your dishes,' so long as you add the correct amount of seasoning (provided in a handy small package), and don't let them dry and burn.

Good of its Kind

That favoured exculpatory phrase on the lines of 'Agreed. It's not very high-brow but at least it's good of its kind' is especially tempting. It seems to avoid the awful business of having to say that some things might be better than others, that some things show the feebleness of their authors' talents and others are no more than market-invented hogwash. In such a world all products should be without distinguishing value-judgements, never set against any other things. All views are horizontal, never vertical. The excusing phrase above is used as a blanket acquittal to avoid any criteria of value being applied, especially to all of what could be called 'the popular arts'. That is a pity because it can have a valid as well as an invalid use.

One could perhaps say of a professional swindler that he or she are 'good of their kind', meaning that they are very successful. If so, perhaps one cannot quarrel with such a judgement; in its own terms. But when most people use that phrase they seem to be implying that that 'good of its kind' is also valid currency outside; that 'good' can be extracted so as to set the swindlers' successful practices on a par with those of a novelist; say, Iris Murdoch. Anyone is free to equate the two levels of 'goodness'; anyone else is free not to equate the achievement of even an extremely popular pop song with *Cosi fan Tutte* or a bestselling pulp novel with *Anna Karenina*; but that is what is implied. We are not here making moral judgements but distinctions of talent. When any judgement of any instance of popular art is declared valid on those 'good of its kind' lines; it is as though it has thus been fenced in, away from external judgement. So you cannot say that a popular novel is feeble because its characterization is wooden, its plot stereotyped and its settings unconvincing. It sold millions so must be good of its kind, hedged from value-judgements which can only be made within its own context; if at all.

A valid use of that 'good of its kind' rule could start by recognizing just what in any particular popular art, other than the numbers who consume it, might actually make it good: verbal or musical inventiveness, say; that might do nicely. Judged in that light it is plain that a great many of today's popular songs fail. Of that, more in the following chapter.

The same rule, it follows, can be applied to some productions which aim to be 'highbrow'. There is false high art in high-flouting novels almost, but not quite, as much as there is in imitation popular art. The scales of value should run from the very top to the very bottom of what is offered at any time, in any genre; but some scales reach higher, and some lower, than others.

Mass art pretends to be wide, all-embracing. It is certainly voluminous, ever-present and continuously renewed. We have seen that it is at the same time a form which, true to its origins, concentrates; that is necessary so that the audiences are closely packed together. It must pack and keep packed as many as possible as that carousel goes endlessly round and round. Branching off, breaking out, to more independent and more qualified opinions (or thoughts) is strongly discouraged. So the narrow focus comes to seem, to express, what all right-thinking people ought to believe; it incites and reinforces by constant repetition. It reinforces above all (with slight variations), mass taste rather than individual judgement, taste in opinions and prejudices as much as in fast foods. It is itself a form of verbal fast food. At the extreme, it may change taste, but even that process cannot come like a bolt from outside. It must latch on to an existing taste. A taste in tastes, perhaps; as in the way hamburgers broke into popular taste – in both senses – by latching on 'to the taste for the "tasty"'. The importance of any thing or event, therefore, is to be assessed by the mass attention given to it; and that attention feeds on itself.

Six Exemplary Deaths

This process is well illustrated by six deaths over the last few years: that, above all, of Princess Diana and then, to a decreasing degree in terms of public response, those of Jill Dando, Paula Yates and Princess Margaret (perhaps those last two were equal-thirds); then, with an interesting upturn, George Harrison, the former Beatle, and finally the Queen Mother.

As to two of these deaths, those of Princess Diana and Jill Dando, it has to be said that the public reaction, no matter how sympathetically it may be viewed, especially from the distance of a few years, was out of proportion to a reasonable assessment of the intrinsic importance of the loss. That is too subjective a statement to be externally proved and will be rejected by the majority, as an unfeeling, out-of-touch and intellectually snobbish judgement. Others might accept the assertion as a statement of the obvious, an indication of the growing superficiality of the mass media, and not worth much further examination; simply another instance of the predominance of head counting as the source of emotional values. That quick dismissal is too easy and misses particular, interweaving and interesting, complexities. 'The heart has its reasons.'

The overwhelming, the hardly suspected, expression of what must be called 'grief' on Princess Diana's death – though what kind of grief it was is another question. It was in one sense public, outside self and family; in another sense it seemed to some people to rank with a death in the family. That evidence of grief astonished anyone who felt to some degree outside it, not superior or cynical, but a watcher, unable or unwilling to take part. What had made the usually undemonstrative British suddenly express loss, and loss outside the family group, in so rhetorical a way? Again, this arose virtually immediately, before the mountainous encouragement of the mass media had got into its stride; these intense feelings for the princess had been building up for years; and a rich mixture they were.

In the light of what has already been argued, and given the way the mass media interact with their audiences, that slightly belated response was so predictable that further examination of the phenomenon might seem hardly worth the effort. That doesn't quite close the issue, though. The reaction in the press, tabloids and broadsheets (in matters such as this the two are coming nearer to each other), on radio and, above all, on television, was all-enveloping. The most important question is one which, again, cannot be indisputably answered but is worth teasing at: how far in all this was the mass media reflecting prior attitudes among the population and how far were they inciting them, or at least increasing them? There is no doubt that Princess Diana held a very complex, extraordinarily widespread and on the whole exceptionally favourable place in the public consciousness. How far had that been formed or enhanced by the mass media before her death? Enhanced almost certainly, over the years; it was always good for extensive treatment. But it also seems likely that in the first place and very much on their own very many people across all classes had 'taken Princess Diana to their hearts'. The Prime Minister's label on her death – 'The People's Princess' – whilst sentimental, touched a truth.

The astonishing reaction could not be said to have either come out of nowhere or been, in a direct or sudden sense, imposed on people. The mass media certainly picked it up and 'ran with it'. But they were able to link their treatment with many attitudes already there, and very widespread, in the public mind. By contrast, before her death many people thought the mass media had cruelly hounded the Princess.

The princess was in a certain way beautiful; she had in addition the allure which good-looking aristocratic women sometimes have; she liked to have a good time and was fond of pop music; she winningly confessed to not being very intellectual or even intelligent; she told one acquaintance that she was 'a bit thick'. But her behaviour after her marriage began to fail was extremely shrewd, indeed closely calculated; she had a warm heart especially towards people in distress or danger – as expressed in her interest in the victims of Aids and her readiness to court danger herself in the effort to outlaw land mines – she was a loving mother; hardly anyone, seeing her passionate rush to embrace her two boys after an absence, could doubt that. She had been ill-used; led, apparently innocently, into a hopeless and, ethically, extremely dubious arranged marriage; she had suffered to the point of attempting suicide when she discovered how emotionally barren the marriage was; she was in some other respects a typical Sloane Ranger, given to health and fitness clubs, smart restaurants and the like. After her marriage broke up she displayed a fatally poor judgement in the men she became attached to, which went with a taste for the expensive high life of large private yachts and prestigious hotels. She could fight hard for her interests and rights; she could be rather silly but she had a big heart and was abused; when she was carrying out her royal duties with 'ordinary people', she almost always seemed genuinely warm and interested, in contrast with some others of the Royals; she had then no starchiness or 'side'. She died in a horrific car accident, like more than one pop star. 'Cover her face, mine eyes dazzle, she died young' would apply better to someone more young and virginal; but has some appropriateness here. Taken as a whole, her entire picture had a fatal – in more than one sense – charisma.

That mixture, and one could add many other contrasting qualities, made her an irresistible figure to many, perhaps most, people of all classes. The mass media had, of course, a good sense of the strength and spread of her popularity but even they, it seems certain, must have been startled by the instant huge response to the news of her death: by the tears in the streets, the hills of flowers. One middle-class writer living in Muswell Hill, that congeries of intellectuals and media people, was surprised when a neighbour of much the same kind drew up in her Volvo station-wagon as he was walking home and said: 'We're taking flowers to Kensington Palace. Aren't you going?' He had not thought of going. That woman was more representative than he was of thousands who came by car, train, taxi, tube, bus, cycle or on foot to lay their wreath or bunch. It was one of the more surprising examples in the whole of the last century of a common impulse moving masses at the same time; the most astonishing outburst of shared emotion since VE Day.

Within hours, of course, the barrage of media coverage began to be laid down. Its main job and purpose was to validate and sustain the outpouring, to assure people that even the most excessive reaction was a proper response to the event. The media were aided by what they decided to see as the Queen's unsuitably slow response to the magnitude of the wholly fitting grief of millions; they made so much of that neglect that one popular commentator suggested the monarchy was threatened. That was a greatly premature implication, neglectful of Buckingham Palace's resilience. The Palace did, after a few days, do something to defuse the criticisms.

All in all, then, events on the death of Princess Diana pyrotechnically illustrated two things: the deep emotional reserves in the British character which can, nevertheless, be brought volcanically to the surface if touched by a personality and event which arouse several deep-seated and contrasting feelings, at once – combining class; wealth; victimization; a girl effectively deserted; a thirst in her admirers for vicarious enjoyment of the ostentatious life; her weakness for passionate attachments to the wrong sort of men; her lack of intellectual interests but possession of a warm heart and one which would court danger when its good instincts were aroused.

The death in bed of Princess Margaret a few years later acted as a low-key coda to that of Princess Diana. At the time of her decision not to marry Group Captain Townsend she was the supreme English female icon. Thereafter she slowly subsided. There was much sympathy for her at first but gradually the more self-regarding aspects of her way of life, apparently with not sufficient counterbalancing characteristics, ensured that she was progressively put to the sidelines. Such reports of her as there were tended to select yet new instances of poor behaviour; in particular her insistence on due protocol. Royalty has to pay its dues and even the usual degree of deference which led many of the mass media to under-report the less attractive aspects of her goings-on did not prevent most people from learning about and making up their minds about these imperfections. It was a sad record but its royal features were as often off-putting as admirable; she ended unable to draw upon more than a few of the qualities which drew a majority to Princess Diana. When Princess Margaret's coffin was borne through the streets of London relatively few gathered to watch it or placed flowers outside her palace home. Spoken and more importantly unspoken comparisons and judgements were being made, and on those judgements Princess Diana weighed enormously more with 'ordinary' people than did the 'real royal', Princess Margaret.

After some rocky years Princess Anne, the Princess Royal, now seems to have quite a warm place in 'the hearts of the people' We will not know until she dies how far she has won her way back. More than Margaret, less than Diana, seems a fair guess.

Princess Diana's grasp on the popular imagination was inevitably manna to the mass media. Even if they had tried, they could not have invented it. It had almost all the ingredients of a successful television soap opera; but it was *real* and that made it compelling. The responses to the deaths of Jill Dando and Paula Yates were both less intense, but each illustrates a way in which the mass media can hook on to and increase the public reaction by calling on not as many but some new and strong interests than did the death of Princess Diana.

Jill Dando was obviously a pleasant, attractive and intelligent woman. The treatment of her murder, since as a media event a murder is even more striking than death in a car crash, was predictably extensive. But even more extensive than might have been predicted; and that can be ascribed to yet another characteristic of the mass media, especially broadcasting and above all television; that is, narcissism. It constantly looks at itself, especially through the images of its own on-screen favourites, and is pleased by what it sees. That conviction is reinforced by the feedback from very many in its audiences whose hunger for 'nice' (and almost as much for, in the right ways, 'nasty') personages is strong. Jill Dando and others in her position gave, as a background reinforcement to her whole public personality, the feeling that she was 'one of us' or, in a favoured cant expression, 'the girl next door'. She seemed to have a level-headed sense of all this, recognized that she did not look 'sexy' and suggested that she gave an expression of 'blandness'. Admirable self-knowledge.

On her death the broadcasters went into full narcissistic – one almost says 'incestuous' – mode; not merely mirroring but also inciting excessive attention in thousands of listeners and viewers. In radio that always involves inviting letters from listeners. On one of the earlier evenings a letter was read, in a suitably treacley, actress's voice, full of the self-serving expressions of unconscious insincerity, which is always indicated by a luxuriating in its own overwhelming sentimentality. A moment's thought should have made the broadcaster managing the programme put it aside; with, no doubt, many others. Instead, it was offered as an admirable expression of 'the nation's' unparalleled and unchallengeable sense of corporate grief; instead of a self-regarding exercise in melancholy whose emotional falsity was no doubt unrecognized even by the writer.

The next day another letter was sober, measured, and critical of excessive media treatment of the death and of the public reaction. It is to the broadcasters' credit, and to their conviction that the interest of balance required this, that the letter was read over the air. But it was read without conviction, or any implication that what it said might be a useful contribution to the public debate. It was presented as though a rather nasty and uncouth (heartless) person had been let into the house out of politeness, but the sooner he left the better. Sentimentality is always easier to project than sober judgement; broadcasters do not like the myths on which they float to be sunk. It would be inflated to talk of a 'conspiracy' between broadcasters and their larger public here; ill-considered unaware complicity will do.

Jill Dando was a 'television personality'; she 'fronted' many shows competently and warmly. She was, to recall Mr Blair, one of the people's sweethearts. The nature of her death was tragic and made to seem the more tragic because its form owed so much to her professional life. 'Personalities', whether in television or others of the mass media, draw the excessive attention of some who are mentally unbalanced. They become, in one of those newly minted words for elements peculiar to our times, the victims of 'stalkers'; sometimes, ultimately, stalkers become murderous.

The process has something of the inevitability of Greek tragedy. But it does not raise supremely important issues about good and evil. It is in the end prosaic and shabby; free of profound moral implications, a meaningless stabbing in a London suburban street by a man out of his mind but fixated on a television-made image. It does not raise great issues about the meaning of life and conduct and the attitude to death. It is, though, almost intolerably sad because of its combination of ordinariness and inflated, tinselly reputation making. The attention given to Ms Dando's death, especially in her own medium, was routinely and depressingly overdone. During that period many people died, some by a criminal act, some accidentally, some at the end of a life of great value to us all, as human beings – through their achievements in medicine or through their great contributions to the betterment of our lives in many other ways. Almost all received little public attention. They would probably have their obituaries in the broadsheets; the tabloids don't go in for that sort of thing, believing it bores their readers. They are probably right in that and no doubt reinforce that attitude.

So there we are: someone who seemed a nice young woman, with a very high public profile, consumed and exploited by all modern means of communication, was killed; and the whole narcissistic machine 'went into overdrive'. The thought of how that would seem to someone in Afghanistan, or Somalia, or in parts of South America or Asia, is chastening. It would throw into relief the shallow quality of our own perspectives. Both Princess Diana and Jill Dando were, in a word much liked today, 'icons'; which used to have a religious meaning but now means any figure whose 'meanings' are, by an acceptance of exaggeration between audiences and media, made into temporary plaster – or plastic – goddesses or gods. All because they died horribly; they had to die to achieve that status. If they had lived and become old the magic sheen would long before have faded. But they might have found something better once the attention had long left them: a happy old age.

Much the same could be said of the death, apparently by overdose, of Paula Yates. An extended examination would add little to what has already been said. She lived like a frenzied butterfly in the world of pop music, she had muddled marriages, she gave her children exotic names, she and her partners used drugs. So she was always a focus of attention for the mass media, she became a fascinating figure heading towards her own destruction. She was destroyed, and given enormously enhanced attention for a few days, then the caravan moved on and she was virtually forgotten; except that someone, somewhere, is probably writing about her life, which will, in turn, be a few day's wonder and then be remaindered. If she was an 'icon', she was a small and brief example of the type; neither the sort of grandeur of Princess Diana nor the televised classic nice girl of Jill Dando. She too was the girl in the next street, but one who fascinated because she was 'no better than she should be', yet still because of all that a favourite subject for gossip.

The attention given to the death of the former Beatle, George Harrison, throws an interesting light on all the former. The public reaction seemed more genuine than one inspired by the media; indeed, it seemed to take most of the media by surprise; once they realized how wide it was, they naturally went into action. A great many people had been moved by his songs and, perhaps even more, by what they saw as his integrity, and especially his search for the good and proper life. Many people seemed to have a sort of wish to understand and be touched by this aspirant towards a kind of peace, grounded in a holy belief. He seemed to have a core of honesty and modesty within him which saved him from the more excessive forms of 'iconization' in his lifetime and on his death. Even though the media did give it a lot of attention, his was not 'a media death' in anything like the full sense. His public achievement and his inner character appeared to suggest to many who had never met him a kind of admirable consonance. This may have been partly an illusion but was born more out of ordinary people's impressions than from what was proposed to them by the mass media. In this sense it may have been a healthier indication of ordinary people's good sense than were some of the reactions to the deaths above; for him, one didn't have to try hard to disentangle the real person and the real reactions from those invented by the mass media.

The news treatment of the Queen Mother's death began with an inflated and disingenuous or plainly foolish accusation that the BBC newsreader on duty had committed an error by not wearing a black tie when making the first announcement. Afterwards the BBC strained to make amends, with substantially flattering programmes about her life. The major arms of the national Establishment enlisted on such occasions spared no effort to make the event seem epochal and organized a suitable response right up to the lying-in-state in Westminster Hall. As foreigners are wont to say: the British do this kind of thing better than any other nation. Large numbers queued to walk past the catafalque; that had its own impressive attraction. The public response did not entirely mirror that organized feeling; the crowds outside were much slighter than those for Princess Diana. Which may not seem surprising given their differences, especially in age. Yet we had been fed year after year with pictures of crowds, mainly middle-aged to elderly women, cheering the old lady as she appeared outside Clarence House. It was all a curious mixture, with the event inflated this time not so much by the mass media as by what one has had to call, for want of a better word, the Royal Establishment. As was to be expected, it took only a few days for more critical pieces – lap of luxury . . . snob . . . runner up of huge overdrafts . . . opinionated right-winger – to appear; though fairly muted in the mass circulation dailies. They have to be careful about when and how far they qualify dreams.

Obscured Censorship

All such excesses, such a plethora of attention to things often of little note, contrast sharply with the more popular mass media's lack of attention to many other things; and not only a lack of attention but a positive turning away from some of these things. This expands a matter just hinted at earlier. The relativist world prides itself on its openness, its freedom from the controls of 'them above'. In fact, as we saw earlier in a related context, it practices its own kinds of censorship; and ironically this censorship is exercised precisely in its dealings with those whom it claims with open arms to serve. It acts as their gatekeeper, keeping out not so much obviously undesirable elements such as rank obscenity or malicious slander but worrying elements, elements which the anonymous audience simply 'might not like' – intellectual criticisms of some popular attitudes, anything remotely judgemental of those attitudes, as well as anything 'arty-farty', which might make readers turn away. In the face of such selectivity, one hears at the back of the mind Milton's bracing question: 'Who ever knew truth put to the worst, in a free and open encounter?'

This is an often hidden but widespread censorship, practised not by stern cardinals or judges but by media operators who confidently feel in their blood a panoramic sense of what people will like and what, on the contrary, will 'put them off'. One typical example from the most evident home of all such practices, the USA, concerns the television version of Dostoevsky's *Crime and*

Punishment. It was a bold and responsible attempt at translation to the small screen of a major novel. But that was incidental to those engaged to buy drama for their American audience. They would see it chiefly as a crime thriller, and those are usually good audience pullers.

It was reported, though, that after agreeing to be partners in the making of the film, the US television company concerned realized that it would show the murder by an axe of an old woman pawnbroker after the first few minutes. To anyone who knew the novel that was the essential opening act because it was committed not by a common criminal but by a student who had part-accepted, part-created his own theory of the total worthlessness of some lives and the privileged worthwhileness of some others. The US television company decided that that would deter many in their audience, which, in turn, would discourage the advertisers. They withdrew from the project.

That is a striking example. Censorship by stealth or implication has many forms which do not rely on specific bannings but work rather by suggestion; suggestion with quiet force for those ready to be influenced. Thus a literary agent reported in 2002 that 'film people' are more and more saying exactly what they want in novels submitted to them as possible films. Not surprisingly; more and more of the publishing world is trammeled in similar ways; big chain booksellers press for larger and larger rebates; agents seek, and often are given, advances on a possible bestseller so large that, without a very expensive promotion, the cost is unlikely to be matched by sales. That too leads to a sort of silent censorship by omission, as many a well-established author is told by his long-standing publisher that it is no longer economic to publish Northern or 'heavy' or some other kinds of novel, as his latest typescript is sent back. Dostoevsky would have had a short answer to that; but it would not have done him much good nowadays. Many others, already realizing that their novels should now be constructions for the market (Aga-sagas, chick lit and the rest), will presumably take the hint and either toe that line or seek one of the new, local, desk-top publishers; and then blush almost unseen, since reviews will be few and advertisements too expensive. Smaller publishers of works unlikely to become bestsellers no matter how expensively they are promoted, but of works they admire and think well worth publishing, find themselves increasingly denied display space by the big booksellers, or even a meeting with the manager. No doubt well-educated and serious readers will discover which small houses cater for them but the opportunities for widening the reading of that kind of book to many others will be reduced.

It is, to run through the sequence again, a collapsing and a concentrating world, a world of no judgements other than those arrived at by head counting, a typical levelling and populist world, an increasingly relativist world. It has produced offspring at various levels and in various forms; from the constricted pattern of bestseller-hunting from agent to publisher to bookseller; to intellectual justifications: 'If people like it, then that's the end of the matter.'

Mutations of Class and Gender

As a result of all the above, is that long-hailed classlessness finally emerging? Not truly. The sense of separateness, of wishing to pull up the drawbridge on those outside and below survives. As to women's clothing, a quick glance may give the impression that the range of new fashion shops has allowed a young woman on a factory conveyor belt or at a supermarket check-out or in a call centre to dress as well as a Sloane Ranger. That is an illusion, and a Sloane Ranger can spot the difference at ten yards. There has been some weakening of older class divisions in cultivated tastes. There are more latter-day Leonard Basts than we recognize but they are still unusual.

Some class habits have been eroded and no doubt more will follow. Some were immensely deep-rooted; more than most other impediments, the combination of class-bound attitudes and male-chauvinism sometimes stood in the way. Immediately after the Second World War the British members of the Special Operations Executive, who had been landed in France at the height of the war to help support and supply the Resistance, were decorated. They had all done valiant work in conditions of great danger; and some paid with their lives, often after torture.

It was astonishing to see, in a film made at the turn into the new century, a parade of women agents who had all been awarded the MBE, the bottom level of the 'British Empire' decorations; and usually awarded to, for example, those who have served faithfully and well in some necessary field (forty years as a postmistress, a midwife or a stalwart in a national charity). They deserve it. But it would be hard to equate their record with that of a resistance fighter facing death month after month; especially since the men involved were given not the MBE nor the OBE nor the CBE, but the much more impressive DSO, membership of the Distinguished Service Order. The DSO (founded in 1886) is a military medal and so not, at that time, available to women. One might have wished that the role of women secret agents in the last war would have prompted a change. Though it was applied half a century ago, the distinction was extraordinary. Was it guided by an unthinking male chauvinism which simply could not conceive that women could equal men in heroism? Even if the terms for the award of the DSO were, in the habitual English way, regarded as immutable, surely the OBE at least, or even the CBE, would have been more fitting than the MBE? Did any of the women refuse it? That would have been understandable. By now, happily, a little of that kind of divisiveness has gone, though whether in the thinking of the military I do not know.

The new society absolutely needs something in place of the traditional class and gender divisions, something which sustains and strengthens it to a degree the old style no longer does. That something is a new style of classification, which might be called compartmentalism, or stratifying, or status charting. In this there are again three divisions, which might suggest that the British cannot give up thinking in threes; or that perhaps there is something deep in human nature which loves a threesome.

Group A is small, perhaps ten per cent, or at the most twenty per cent, of the population. Membership is not usually decided by birth or attendance at a major public school; it is, rather, the home of the meritocrats. Its typical professions include, of course, Information Technology, and then Communications of many kinds, and all areas where the movement of money is involved. Group A is therefore wide open to accessions from below. It does not subsequently lose as many members as did the old upper class since it has fewer who are there by the simple chance of birth, which meant that some were not very bright and, unless supported from within, probably sank. Group A is now much entered not by class of origin but by a combination of brains and education. Its members' high salaries make it worth servicing by the mass media. Group A members, taken together, do not make a mass audience, but individually have more to spend than the average member of Group B. Add the developments in media technology, which lower the numbers needed to make a profit, and provision for the high-level tastes of Group A becomes relatively attractive; as many small circulation technical and professional journals illustrate. So do the customers for Waterstones and other new-style bookshops, the range of expensive foreign holidays and cruises, mail-order wine clubs and the choice of Waitrose over Tesco (though that has by now successfully blurred the class composition of its customers). Other offerings, especially advertisements for home and gardening extravagancies, are most easily to be found in the back pages of the glossier expensive magazines.

Group C is small, perhaps about ten percent. It is composed of the long-term unemployed, the only just employable at the minimum wage or lower (as happens quite widely), the underclass. There is little specific provision for them unless one includes the magazine the *Big Issue* which, at the time of writing, is threatened with failure. But with that there is probably by definition a gap between those people (especially the underclass) and those issues with which it concerns itself and those who actually buy and read it. For the big battalions among the media of communication there is likely to be little profit from a frontal advertising or P. R. assault on these lowest of people. They are hardly worth tempting. They are left to booze and drugs and virtually hopeless hopes from the National Lottery; or they fight as best they can against the drudgery of poverty ('keeping our heads above water'), especially among that major sub-group within the total: the one-parent families, that one usually a woman.

Group B is, of course, the really big group, the solid majority. Most are not in Group A because they do not have one of the necessary forms of advanced education. Most of them do have that new phenomenon, discretionary money at the end of each week. They include many who used to call themselves 'working-class', and some among them may still do so, as a sort of residual class pride or disinclination to adopt any of the other traditionally tainted labels. Many have moved from the old heavy industry, working-class districts and bought a privately built semi. They include many who used to belong to the lower middle-class, and some perhaps feel they still do. Most are not highly educated; but many possess different levels of craft skills rather than scientific or advanced technological training. The lists include people in low-level but on the whole steady work and move upwards to qualified craftsmen and technicians, usually short of tertiary-level education in technology or a science. They make up about seventy-five to eighty per cent of the population. Few join them from below in spending power but many from Group C do join them in those leisure pursuits which are free; in watching television but not in going regularly to football matches, or to ten-pin bowling, both of which are neither free nor cheap. No such divisions are watertight. Many from Group A relax watching manifestly Group B programmes such as 'Blind Date'; even more share Group B and C's love of football (on television for Group C). Group B is so large as to merit subdividing: for example, one segment of Group B is the target for bestsellers, from thrillers through airport novels to what could still be called 'middlebrow' reading.

The major separation in the choice of newspapers survives; except that some of the broadsheets seem to be going down market, perhaps because, for money's, sake they want to broaden their readership so as to make themselves more secure. For some, advertising revenue is falling damagingly, and the internet poses an increasing threat. Or perhaps they move into the upper levels of Group B because their existing readers are believed to be lightening and lowering their tastes. It is easy to understand the pressures; the drive to maintain or increase circulation is insistent and pressing; in this jungle, relativism justifies a 'more democratic' spread in readers. So the senior executives are driven by a combination of nervously looking over their shoulders at the competition and the belief that the old-style, identifying grouped readership can be virtuously broadened. Similarly, the old-style English suspicion of evident intellect ('too clever by half') plays its part. It is to the *Guardian*'s credit that in 2002 it launched the Literary Review committed to high literary standards, not to market-chasing.

The centre of Group B marks the prime aim of the marketers and their minions. Its members have more to spend than those of Group C but most have not as much spare money as do most members of Group A. But there are so many of them that they easily constitute the largest money-target of all; they must therefore have most attention.

The old sense that there have to be divisions, now of status if not of class, survives and reinvents itself, especially with some railway companies. Once a passenger with a cheap day return ticket mixed with all others paying full 'standard fares' (another levelling word, to avoid labelling anyone 'second class'). One company now uses separate coaches for the two and provides tea or coffee for the 'full standard' passengers. Once for a small supplement you could travel first class at weekends. Now, for a supplement into the tens of pounds (it is regularly increased) you can travel in a first-class coach but not be a first-class passenger; they are in one coach still reserved for *real* first-class passengers, who have extra treats.

I was once, because my host there had bought such a ticket for me in advance, obliged to travel by business class to Belfast in the middle of the day, with the British Midland airline. The difference in price between economy and business class was great. Between refreshments the difference was not noticeable, very light indeed for all. There was considerable delay on the way out. On the return journey our flight was cancelled due, we were told, to weather conditions; British Airways was still taking off. A world-weary fellow traveller suggested that, as an economy when aircraft were only lightly booked, British Midland would cancel some flights and put their waiting passengers on the next one; if that is so, it is not helpful to passengers due to make connections at Heathrow. The delay lengthened and I attempted to enter the business class lounge. A brusque young woman barred my way. Apparently only those who have travelled 'x' times, not merely once, by British Midland's business class and can wave a stamped card of proof – Green Shield stamps born again – are qualified for entry. The British capability for inventing nit-picking social distinctions is inexhaustible; and sickening. Other dispiriting things during that one trip made me unlikely to use that airline again. A letter to their P. R. department produced a brush-off; so their treatment of customers was consistent.

As we have seen, if occasions require it, 'stratification' can take a series of different forms. In some, it produces new areas for divisiveness, decided not by class but by the pressures of commerce. In fact, the traditional class-divided society in some important issues also overrode its divisions and acted as one: as in the uniform cost of postage across the United Kingdom, and the founding, or the impulse behind the founding, of the National Health Service; and in many aspects of insurance.

One of the early deviations from that principle was the moving away of private (paid) medical care from the national service. At the time of writing the uniform rate of postage is threatened as that service is to become part-privatized. Insurance services are in some respects the most striking example of the new stratification. One company really doesn't want to hear from you, whether for personal or motor car cover, if you are above a certain age; nor will your house be insured if it is more than a surprisingly low number of years old, and may be more solidly built and better maintained than most modern houses. The rules are clear and absolute since they must be capable of being accurately transmitted by the galley slaves of the call centres. By such methods a firm narrows the range and size of likely claims. It can lower its rates, attract young customers in young houses, and make larger profits. The older in old houses pay more. No doubt someone feels very proud of inventing that procedure.

These new kinds of subdividing take less obvious forms. As we have seen, most popular quiz shows are founded on populist levelling, in the firm unuttered conviction that all are equal, that levelling is a democratic exercise. Hence the sequences of questions which could only be successfully answered by someone with an unordered, undiscriminating, magpie brain, since they range from asking the name of the second drummer in an obscure pop group to who was Don Quixote's servant or, even harder, who wrote *The Ambassadors*? They are not except tangentially looking for magpies, though are pleased occasionally to attract a spectacular member of the breed. They are doing the opposite: fending off, making sure that their questions do not demand a uniformly and seriously well-stocked mind or a mind capable of difficult thinking on its feet. Clever clogs like those would damage the levelling instinct, and ensure that a bird-brain is not shown up, by virtually ensuring that the well-stocked brain is floored by such as that pop drummer question. A fall assumed to be relished.

Who Wants to be a Millionaire? is the archetype of such programmes. *The Weakest Link* takes the form unpleasantly further. *Millionaire* is cosy and comforting; the *Link* is rude and can be painful to those discarded, because it makes them feel small. A friend who had been a victim of Nazi anti-Semitism phoned after seeing *The Weakest Link* for the first time, in some disquiet. 'I've just seen my first Nazi programme on BBC television,' he said. His nerves were probably more sensitive to harshness than those of most of us but he had a strong point. Even though many millions watch that programme, it is still a disgrace to a civilized society and no reiterations of the usual excuses ('Only a bit of fun', 'No-one takes it seriously' and so forth) can remove that condemnation. Ann Robinson's typical signing-off sums it up: 'YOU have won – £1500. And YOU have won – NOTHING. Goodbye!' The latest example of that disreputable breed is: 'Test the Nation; the National 2002 Test', which had almost two and a half hours of evening screening time on BBC1. It was lowering to its audience, its participants, its presenters and producers; a gross waste of a useful medium. Has the BBC, in putting on such programmes, lost every sense of the good uses of that medium?

It is a pity but typical that University Challenge, which might have been expected to exhibit the finest young brains battling against each other in trying to answer important questions, is shot through with questions which test little but the memory of things not worth remembering. The pop drummer again. The fact that, in the knowledge that such questions do appear, the teams usually take care to include at least one member who has just that knowledge proves nothing worthwhile, is only a sign that choice follows expectations good or bad; in this instance, bad. When one does see good minds in action, whether or not they know the drummer's name, it shows what is being lost, and is no guide to the success of their teams; there are always other drummers to be remembered.

Against all this there seems to linger a taste, a sort of hidden hunger which we looked at earlier from another angle; that out of all the quietly heaving but essentially levelling sea, a solitary something or someone different, distinctive, will emerge. Not someone cleverer, of course; someone lucky in the way the questions fall, perhaps; or someone in all other ways nice and ordinary but, yes, with an unthreatening vast ragbag of the mind, one of those jackdaws but an exceptionally glossy one.

A final summary of the argument so far; we move from head counting, through levelling and populism to relativism; these are among the main guiding-forces of today. It is not odd that, given these criteria, McDonald's hamburgers are the pinnacle of culinary standards, of taste; much better than a meal prepared by a three-star chef since so many more millions have voted for it with their mouths. Challenged, many would probably say that, yes, they do prefer a McDonald's burger to all that fancy stuff. The difference can't be proved, as we have said again and again, any more than can the superiority of one author to another; and McDonald's offerings are indisputably and always and everywhere 'tastier'. That's the point and the power.

So what can we do, individually and collectively? Draw upon our ironic, mickey-taking, bloody-minded spirit. Bombard all the offenders with criticism; and praise as needed. Never join the big battalions. Try to think for ourselves. Mock disguised censorship and phony language. Try to act like free citizens, not subjects or dupes.

Chapter 4

Celebrities, Sponsors, Youth

'Fashions, after all, are only induced epidemics.'
(G. B. Shaw, Preface to *The Doctor's Dilemma*)

I have told this incident in an earlier book but it is too apt to omit here. One morning in Farnham's main street a sizeable crowd, mainly of women, filled the pavement outside a chocolate shop about to open for the first time. Squeezing past, I asked one of them what the occasion was. 'Oh, Vanessa's in there, signing autographs.' Up to that time I had not heard of Vanessa Feltz, a frequent performer on daytime television.

That little occasion is worth recalling for one of its elements. The woman did not say: 'Vanessa Feltz'. She simply assumed that I, an elderly man and, if she had noted my way of speaking, not likely to be a Vanessa fan, would recognize her by her first name. She is a 'celebrity'.

What is a celebrity, that title so much favoured today? The word is above all a loose, capacious bag which finds room for not only Royalty, and film stars (star is still in use, though almost restricted to the cinema – celebrity is now much preferred), but also, at different points on a scale of popularity, for television people from actors to newscasters and weather presenters, for cooks/chefs (male and female, black, white, rude, comical, rough working-class, smooth and elegant), for top-class footballers, and many others. In Britain the word is not often heard in reference to, say, a Nobel prizewinner, or about most others who have made some advance in the work of the mind; France's *Le Monde* records the death of one of the country's leading sociologists, at length and prominently on the front page. An English broadsheet put on its front page at about the same time a large portrait of the widow of a television star, attending his memorial service.

The marriages of commoners into Royalty over the last couple of decades has given the mass media a particularly difficult but succulent bone to chew. Some merge from the start into a virtually anonymous background and stay there largely left alone by journalists (Princess Anne's husband, Tim Lawrence), some provide lots of scandalous copy by behaving in a distinctly un-Royal way (including the Duchess of York), another actually belongs to the P. R. world and has exhibited some of its less attractive characteristics (The Countess of Wessex). But then, to some extent they had their earlier models in the Duke of Edinburgh and Prince Charles, both presenting the mass media from time to time with particularly difficult materials: private lives to chew over with delightedly raised eyebrows, but all running together with some residual deference, the old respectfulness for a Queen's Consort and a Crown Prince.

One of the most glowing marks of celebrity status is given to those who exhibit a special skill, especially in sport and even more so in football. This admiration for football is widespread through the classes; a weekly political columnist in one of the broadsheets will happily report on a visit to his favourite team. Plainly, many of the crowd do recognize the finer points of the game; the often brutish and xenophobic behaviour of a minority suggests that their main interest is simply the actual scoring of goals by 'our side'. The irony is that because of the increasing competitiveness and commercialization of the game, and as a team becomes more prosperous, 'our side' is to a considerable extent composed of bought-in foreigners. 'Local loyalty' takes on a new meaning. When a player, native or foreign, goes to an even more lucrative post with another team, the grandstands sprout 'Judas' placards; that is one literate reference; though a logically wobbly one.

Celebrity overlaps with personality but is not the same, is publicly less though in true definition certainly not less; more, rather. We say 'she is a celebrity' meaning she is very well known publicly; which means much treated in 'celebrity' magazines such as *O.K.* and *Hello*, the popular press and television. We can also say not merely 'she is a personality' but 'she has a really strong personality' and that refers to inner character. A celebrity may have a weak, pusillanimous character, so that one would be unlikely to say of her 'she's got real personality'. We are aware underneath that the title of celebrity is bestowed on someone by their audience; personality more often inheres in, belongs to the wearer, as observed from outside.

Personality often suggests a marked charisma and that is usually, but not always, favourable. A personality may radiate good sense, strong will and effectiveness; or something very different. A very well-known model is of course a celebrity even if she shows an unpleasant personality when she exploits her celebrity by, as was reported of one, telling the doorman at a reception, who had asked her to stop smoking before entering, that he could 'fuck off', and continuing to smoke. Luckily, the first kind of personality (the admirable) seems more common than the second; or perhaps that is no more than a pious wish. Having or being a personality is linked with having a character or even 'being a character'; but by then we are moving away from the artificial world of celebrities into the real and ordinary world. We would be slightly startled to hear that a certain female model, and hence a celebrity, was also 'a real character'; that suggests a distinctive personality, probably some worldly wit, and then threatens to release the celebrity from her remote, non-worldly pedestal into the world of thoughtful conversation. A female model who had a 'bad character', was self-centred and abusive to those around her, would not fall from her plinth. That can go with her job and add to her interest.

In this area we are today particularly fond of successive key-words. We have seen that we like 'icon' far too much; it also goes into that capacious bag, but with a difference. An icon is no longer a religious object but another kind of representative figure, standing for something usually secular, representing some important movement or feeling within society; and on the whole is in that a good symbol, but sometimes neutral and occasionally 'a bad example'. 'Role model' can take the place of 'icon', but is more down-to-earth and ambiguous. Talking on the radio today about a footballer in trouble with the law, a fan said rather aggressively in his defence: 'Still, he is a role model.' Both 'role model' and 'icon' should by now be given a rest. They have been used and misused too long and have become loose, like wobbly old statues.

'Diva', which was recently and surprisingly attached to an international supermodel, is the Italian word for an operatic *prima donna*. A further look shows that Italians may also use it insultingly and more widely, to mean an arrogant woman. We do not use it in that sense, though it fitted where it was applied to an English model, as here. We might normally have said *prima donna*, even among working-class people – 'She's a real *prima donna*, she is.'

Still, that wider use of role model is intriguing. It is clearly meant in most instances to indicate a good, a worthwhile, model to follow; but some people today use it even more widely than the person quoted above and will without ambiguity say of a young criminal that his role model is an older practitioner, a celebrated crook. This is an interesting instance of a word losing its ethical penumbra so as to be used freely in a society which recognizes few ethical principles.

Celebrity can absorb but should not be confused with 'model' on its own, usually meaning a woman – though naturally there are male models – who 'models' new and fashionable and expensive clothes. It sometimes seems as though this group, especially its main branch that of the 'international superstar' models, inspires more media attention than any other single type of celebrity. They are striking to look at if not always beautiful; their most common stance, no doubt worked out by their manager and the photographers, is slightly at an angle to the camera, one hand on the sideways-bent left hip as though it needs support, and the eyes quite looking away from that part of the body as though it doesn't concern them. At bottom the total effect is all of manner, not of matter.

That effect also requires severe selection; of characteristics, actual or invented, which will make up not a rounded, three-dimensional personality, but a particularly fascinating two-dimensional figure composed of elements which, whilst retaining the sense of distance and of the high life, also hint at touches of extraordinary-ordinariness: she likes hamburgers and walking on the beach without shoes.

Here again, there enters that narcissism which was noted in the last chapter as particularly common in television. Catwalk personalities appear, when on the catwalk, as profoundly narcissistic. They are now no longer turned away from the camera, looking away from their own bodies, but are turned in on them; wrapped up within themselves, within their expression, their stance, their creams and perfumes and overall make-up. They are as if stroking themselves or at least their *personae*, totally immersed in professional self-regard. 'Because I'm worth it.' This narcissism has been broadened by the advertisers to women in general: 'Because you're worth it', 'Be good to yourself', 'You owe it to yourself', 'The closest shave that every girl deserves', and, about the effects of a perfume, 'YOU made it happen'. The Labour Party manifesto urged that we vote for them: 'Because you deserve better'. All this picks-up from American advertising in the 1950s, after behavioural scientists had put themselves at the service of the advertising trade. At the back echoes the reverse: 'When a man takes a wife, he finds out whether/Her knees and elbows are only glued together.' That is not male chauvinism, only a recognition that in hard days a marriage can collapse, and a home and family, if wife and husband don't work as one.

So it is not felt that catwalk models need be friendly, in the way that is expected of most types of television personalities; models can be aloof or even unpleasant, known to be 'no better than they should be', perhaps 'into drugs'. The entire effect is often rather louche and distant; cold, uncaring; of someone far 'too hard to get', all expression and impression; so that one cannot easily imagine them in the matrimonial bed or getting the children off to school with their hair still in curlers. Naturally, some can be pleasant enough or, if the life of celebrity and the money have gone to their heads, willful and unpleasant. Some decades ago they were known as 'mannequins' but that word has now fallen into complete disuse. For older people mannequins will bring back memories of the then 'smart and fashionable' clothes from Marshall and Snelgrove, and the limited range of popular perfumes which went with them; but mannequins were hardly ever celebrities; one could imagine them packing their bags in the back of the Department Store and going home to the suburbs, sometimes to Mum and Dad; or being picked up by their boyfriends in an M.G.

This common hauteur or apparently required sense of aloofness given off by many celebrity-models recalls yet again, but by contrast, those television personalities looked at earlier, such as Jill Dando, and nowadays Carol Smillie (surely a pseudonym, or coincidence has become almost unbelievable). When one thinks of such people, the old expression: 'Oh, she/he is all smiles' comes to mind, a phrase which sometimes, but not always, hints at hypocrisy. The operetta *The Land of Smiles* can be heard in the background; as a fitting theme tune for much television. Obviously those permanent smiles, sometimes more like grins, are much valued as tone setters, mood establishers, expression fixers, friendly wrap arounds for almost any kind of programme. Their wearers must usually be 'good-lookers' in a conventional sense, or occasionally *jolie-laide*, and 'good pros', since some are required to 'front' a remarkable range of programmes, from the vapidly amusing to the demandingly serious. The wonder is then that 'one small head can carry all she knew' – which it doesn't – she learns it for the day and time or follows the autocue. On the whole one wishes that directors would be less fixed in the conviction that programme chocolate-wrappers such as those are almost essential to 'get across' any kind of programme; and are particularly helpful if the programme qualifies as public service broadcasting, since that is widely thought to equate with 'dull and taxing'. So the broadcasters too, especially in television, are narcissistic in their constant presentation of minor and temporary celebrities – what they eat, where they live and with whom. The *Radio Times* endorses this deep-rooted institutional narcissism and so do the many other TV magazines. Some families are absorbed by interest in it.

Those smiles becomes types of rictus since the bearers know that above all, and though some are also intelligent and articulate, it is the smile-capacity which recommends them to the planners. Incidentally, it seemed slightly off-target for a well-known television woman journalist to complain that experienced but by now early middle-aged members of that corps were being ousted by others with cute or tight little bottoms. Surprising are those younger members often shot from behind; surely the near-permanent frontal smiles dominate? There are plenty of bottoms in *Top of the Pops*, but not those of journalists.

'Fame is the spur.' Another word within this general cluster, but one now comparatively little used or used almost wholly in a rather narrow sense, is: 'famous'. Of course any Celebrity will be famous; the earlier word is then contained within the later; and of course a famous person (not 'Famous Personality' – that would seem slightly tautologous since the second word again contains the first; or, more likely, the union straddles uneasily two different cultural and linguistic worlds) a famous person will surely be well known. Both 'famous' and 'well-known' belong to a more sober, less crowd-driven world. You may become famous for some achievement, in the first instance recognized by your peers or colleagues; you can be well known in your city for good works; celebrity and even at times personality belong to the wider, more hyped, world. They have nothing to do with the hiding of lights under bushels; nor are they associated with the long and worthwhile haul. Those belong to another world of judgement, much of it felt in the mind without being often uttered.

Instances from the nineteenth century can be intriguing: 'While I was in London, the melancholy death of Lord Byron was announced in the public papers . . . The common people felt his merits and his power, and the common people of a country are the best feelings of a prophecy of futurity.' That was John Clare in 1824.

In 1850 Macaulay described in a letter to a friend, after having it from Thackeray, a moving moment. There were at the time queues at the zoo to see the strange new animal, the hippopotamus: 'Thackeray swears that he was eyewitness and ear-witness of the proudest event of my life. Two damsels were just about to pass that doorway which we, on Monday, in vain attempted to enter, when I was pointed out to them. "Mr Macaulay" cried the lovely pair, "Is that Mr Macaulay? Never mind the hippopotamus." And having paid a shilling to see Behemoth, they left him at the very moment at which he was about to display himself to them, in order to see – but spare my modesty.'

In such an instance comparisons can be very tricky, but can go some way. Perhaps those who could afford a shilling in 1850 (later reduced to 6d) were largely middle-class and upwards, and so the girls were, perhaps, educated and well read. The first two volumes of his *History of England,* issued in 1849, had made Macaulay – avoiding the word 'celebrity' – celebrated. The young ladies were well aware of that, as well perhaps, as it was not a very good year for new English fiction, of the publication in that year of the latest of Browning's poems, the almost impenetrable 'Sordello'. Their lack of hesitation in giving up the hippopotamus in favour of a heavyweight writer is still surprising. Macaulay himself seems surprised and proud by his new-found fame and its remarkable spread. What would be the modern equivalent? Giving up queuing to see the first panda in captivity because T. S. Eliot appeared nearby? That seems unlikely though possible. Much more likely is that young ladies of any class would leave the queue only if a celebrity such as Paul McCartney appeared.

Inevitably, those subspecies mentioned earlier are parasitic on the emergence of mass-media celebrities: the paparazzi with their long-distance lenses and no-holds-barred attitude, and those reporters who hang around airplane exit tunnels at Heathrow to accost celebrities known to be booked on certain flights; and, lowliest of all, those who chase after police vans taking the latest celebrity – that is, notorious criminal – to jail. It seems as though modern, 'developed' societies need as much as their predecessors famous people of many sorts and at all times. People to 'look up to'? Yes, sometimes; but, as we have seen, that is not greatly relevant to today's cult of the personality. Being infatuated by a model with the fame of Kate Moss is not 'looking up to' her, except in a material sense, but shows a huge yearning interest in learning everything possible about people whose lives are so different from ours, so 'glamorous'; so much the material for *Hello* and *O.K.* Hopelessly distant from us but that fact does not make the fans sad; it increases their avidity.

It would be easy to ascribe this 'not looking up to but being fascinated by the otherness of a few' to a change in many

Celebrities, Sponsors, Youth

people's attitudes starting somewhere in the twentieth century, probably from roughly its middle. The changes described elsewhere in these pages go some way towards explaining such alterations in attitudes. But the urge to be fascinated (which may or may not include 'looking up to' someone in the ethical sense) by the lives of people quite out of reach, grander, more glamorous, exotic has long been there in most of us. Interest in the doings of the Royal family, favourable or not, is a clear and continuing instance of that; though now, in part but strongly, sustained (since so many other examples have begun to seem at least as interesting) by occasions when members of that family misbehave – most astonishingly in the audio-taped revelation of intimacies between the Prince of Wales and his mistress. From this perspective the peculiarities of the twentieth century-onwards love of the celebrity has emerged from that of previous centuries, chiefly as a necessary component of the mass society and the mass media. We are back yet again with the vast increase in available, freely disposable, money across almost all levels of society; with the technological ability to attract that money, and the willingness of many often gifted people to service those – avoiding the word 'profession' – occupations. This combination of elements and forces is, paradoxically, all the greater when for most of the time and across most of society there are offered very few other markers, especially markers to 'look up to'. That phrase has now come to mean 'immensely attractive to large numbers of people' through a considerable mixture of responses; which may not include many drawn by admiration for virtue of character. The replies of the 'men and women in the street' during the celebrations of the Golden Jubilee proved that a great number, perhaps even a majority, still hold that generalized 'looking up to' feeling for royalty. A vacuum is again being filled.

It follows that many of the celebrities most active within the mass media exhibit more and more a sort of class or region-free accent and emerge with what is rather dubiously called 'estuary

91

speech' (dubious because that type of speech belongs less to geography, more to culture and occupation).

In such a world, popular representative expressions such as: 'famous for being famous' encapsulate the final emptiness and brevity of many choices of celebrities, as does: 'soon everyone will be able to be famous for fifteen minutes', which calls up the expanding vistas of accidental, brief, manufactured fame about virtually anything which seems worth one day's headlines, one day's door-stopping, one day's paparazzi pursuit. Then, away.

Sponsors

We need now to come back to sponsorship; this time from a different angle, that of those who agree to undertake sponsorship and promotions through advertising. They include celebrities of many kinds, especially key celebrities of the time: and, even more particularly, television actors and personalities and top-level professional footballers.

There are a few, a very few, who refuse the large sums of money offered if they will engage in commercial sponsorship. I know of two actors who have done that; they do not use the product to be plugged and, even if they did, cannot make informed comparisons with it and others in that area. I also know a journalist who is not a celebrity in the most 'celebrated' sense but is known and respected by an informed audience. He refused to advertise, for a substantial fee, the merits of the business class of an airline. He argued to himself that his premier professional claim rested on the assumption of his readers that what he wrote he honestly believed to be true; he would have irretrievably damaged that if he made claims he could not substantiate by relevant comparisons, but had been paid to assert.

This may certainly puzzle most of those who have taken the money, many of them at the top of the tree. Questioned, one agent said that a celebrity who was outstanding could command

£500,000 and well beyond, and that £100,000 was not uncommon. Some will think it holier than thou to take up an ethical position especially today when, as we have abundantly seen already, to offer any decision on a judgement of value, is becoming increasingly 'not worth making a fuss about'. They simply do not see why they should not take the money and buy that weekend cottage in the country. It seems not to occur to them, as they praise foods they have probably not eaten or stores they do not patronize, that they are misusing their voices and faces for gain; and, more, are deceiving many who have come to admire them for fine acting and now may be tempted to accept what they say without question. Perhaps some comfort themselves by feeling that, even in their roles as actors, they are being used, paid, to be what they are not. So why make over-fine distinctions? Talking about the experience of filming, one actor said bitterly: 'You're such a commodity.'

Most actors (though not the ones most often invited to undertake television advertisements, the most successful and prosperous) will point out that they are 'resting', drawing the dole, more often than acting; sponsorship money can save them from near-penury. That can be true and one understands the pressure and the temptation. Some, as was noted above, do resist as a matter of principle. Each answer must be an individual's. One can only hope that that answer is arrived at after more thought than seems usual; beginning with looking at the professional irresponsibility of warmly putting claims whose truth you have not at all questioned, about a product you may have hardly heard of until the adman called. It would be interesting to know – perhaps they will tell us – whether the Board of Equity have ever addressed the issue; that seems doubtful.

What if, after your promotion has appeared, its claims about a butter-substitute or a breakfast cereal or a Finance House prove to be exaggerated or ill-founded, would you then question your own judgement in agreeing to appear in the advertisements?

Would others take note and question you? Would your public impact be lessened? I suspect the answer to all three questions would be 'no', or 'hardly at all'.

In 2001 an interesting coda was added to this matter. A young woman sailed her yacht single-handedly round the world. On return she was of course greeted ecstatically by a large crowd; including those wanting her to sign extremely lucrative sponsor-ship deals. She refused. A BBC interviewer, a very intelligent woman, challenged her, plainly puzzled, almost incredulous. She apparently saw nothing in the slightest degree questionable about taking sponsorship money of that sort. The yachtswoman replied simply that she had all the aid – modest sponsorship of a relevant kind – that she needed. The interviewer found it diffi-cult to cope with that kind of answer; it was so much outside the usual boundaries, by introducing an ethical choice – refusing riches, or at any rate a more well-fed backing for her next voyage. From outside one does not know what, if any, other than that simple statement about not needing more, were then in play with her. Some time later, it appeared that she was accepting more sponsorship. Perhaps she had found that for what she wished to do next she was badly under-funded; or had she succumbed? One can hear the encouraging voices: 'Everybody's doing it now.'

Perhaps the failure which most summed up the moral am-biguity which can surround advertisements, actors, and real life was that of the previously highly-regarded insurance company *Equitable Life*. It ran a series of brilliant advertisements on tele-vision in which a manifestly middle- to upper-middle class, elderly gent, obviously living easy and comfortable, was in the garden with his grandson. The punch-line from grandfather to grandson, delivered in fruity and cultivated tones, was: 'It's an Equitable Life, Henry.' Equitable Life was much liked by people of that status or aspiring to it; it gave unusually good terms for, among other offerings, retirement pensions. That promotion was, it seems likely, in its own terms a winner. A year or so later

Equitable Life collapsed; the market had worsened; it could not maintain its promised terms. There followed many months in which people tried to recover something of what they had expected but now would probably not receive, or not in full.

The story is worth telling because it gathers together so much of the burden of this section. An advertising agency, without actually promising any concrete result financially, produced a script which, very well acted, had immense powers of *suggestion*, which is the main gateway to persuasion. If it had the desired effect on potential customers, they would be won over, and existing customers reassured though, to repeat, it made no actual promises but merely surrounded the words 'Equitable Life' with an unspecific but strong confident middle-class halo of promise. Surveying the subsequent disaster and the thousands of damaged pensions, one wonders whether the advertising agency, the actors and the officers of Equitable Life have had any second thoughts about the desirability of the promotion; I should guess not. Probably they would all be surprised by the question. After all, they live in 'the Real World', don't they?

The obsession with celebrities was also well illustrated by a campaign against Britain going over to the Euro. A parade of celebrities, both major and minor, appeared on screen saying that such a move was wrong. The silliest was one invoking Hitler. Any attempt at serious thought about whether we should make the change was unlikely to be influenced by such cack-handed advertisements. Anyone who took them seriously is unlikely to vote anyway. An own goal.

All this world – of celebrities, their agents, their advertisers and the firms which employ them – belong centrally to today's relativist world and, within that, to populism. That world must be served by a procession of at bottom bland, apparently classless, people (though there is space for stock characters who exude 'local colour'). Where they are required to speak, they must have neither a troubling voice nor disturbing opinions; they must have 'the correct opinions for the time of year'; they are mirrors, focused at first on existing popular taste.

This hidden pressure not to utter disagreeable opinions, spreads everywhere, even to the groves of academe, if we can seriously use that phrase today. One distinguished academic gives high praise to the verse of George Harrison of the Beatles, as though they are to be spoken of in the same breath as those of George Herbert. Another equally well-known academic says that Bob Dylan is as good a versifier as Keats.

This is the inspiration behind all those routines mockings at High Court judges who reveal ignorance of, for example, the latest number one pop group. They might know of such groups and all their surroundings, if they happen to be interested in such things or feel that to understand them might sometimes help them with their work. But they do not *have* to be acquainted with them or their kind, or anything associated with them. There is much else they could become profitably acquainted with relevant to their profession. They do need knowledge of the mass media world sometimes, in their day-to-day work; they can soon acquire it; they do not have to live within that world, as so many people so profitably do. Better to read a good book – say, *Bleak House* or *Crime and Punishment* – or any other which might help them reflect on the good, the true and the beautiful; and perhaps to let those throw reflections on their work.

One judge recently stood up briskly (or 'robustly', in the current jargon) for his right to judge the world in his own best way. Counsel had tried to buttress his case by saying that X, a woman celebrated for giving her views on television and radio, had spoken in support of the case he was defending. He obviously thought that that quoted opinion would weigh considerably with the judge. Whether the judge had or had not heard of the celebrated lady is beside the point. He merely replied that he did not at all care what was X's opinion in this matter; it would be set aside. One might well imagine that some at least among the jury would find it extraordinary that the opinion of one so well-known, so much a celebrated utterer of what so many assume to be weighty opinions, should be brushed aside in that way. It would be like not knowing who Vanessa Feltz was. The judge was of course declaring that he did not belong nor wish to belong to the world of relativist-populism by celebrity soundbites.

A recent large gathering at the Royal Academy to celebrate the Queen's Jubilee mirrored all this. The spread of what was felt to include 'artists' was wider than the Great Bed of Ware; anything to avoid a suggestion of elitism. It will be interesting to see, in ten years time, how many of those 'celebrity artists' will have survived in informed, or public, opinion. Before then, with luck, some of them might be invited to appear in television's latest daft idea: 'Celebrity Boxing'.

Youth

The most persistent double deceit practised on young people by the mass media is: they are fed according to the assumed tastes of their age group; at the same time they are prepared to become adults already primed for being handed over to the later persuaders.

It is deeply unfashionable, especially in an old person, to say anything in criticism of what can rightly be called the Cult of Youth. They are 'old dogs in the manger', 'spoil-sports who never remember being young themselves'. That group is led not only by young entrepreneurs but by older people whose occupation it is to welcome the Cult of Youth, sometimes out of sentiment, more often to relieve young people of their spare money. To put up that welcoming banner in many solemn meetings of adults has become yet another totemic act, a sign of good sentiment. At one point someone is bound to interject: 'but have we thought about the needs of youth?', even if those needs are irrelevant or have already, though not requiring to be made explicit, been provided for.

In discussing pop songs or other aspects of that kind of pop culture it is necessary to distinguish it from 'Pop Art' as associated with the work of Richard Hamilton and Peter Blake; that can be explorative. The elements of pop music as it directs itself at young people are essentially transient. And classless? To some extent; that too is part of its derivative nature, its role within the mass media and their powerful thrusts.

Certainly, pop music is worth examining; but it is not necessary, indeed it is a block to understanding, if total and uncritical immersion takes place; as does happen. Today a putative intellectual position is capable of assertions such as: 'Historically, popular culture will be seen as more important than two world wars'. That comes from the outer, free-floating fringes of a university's course on the mass media. Behind the error of judgement, one might just see a tiny element of truth. At bottom, the author is aiming to make the case for serious study of the mass media rather than instant dismissal of the subject as inconsiderable. So far so good, but he then goes off on to a ludicrous comparison. His error is fundamental and one which any useful work in this area must at all costs and early avoid: he fails to see that much (not all) pop music can be studied as *representative* of elements in modern society, not as *creative criticisms* of it. They are examples rather than exemplary; they do tell us something about that society and so are worth looking at closely; they never stand outside society and cast a beady eye on it. This is true of most 'revolutionary' pop songs; in their contexts they become examples of 'permitted deviations', and are soon taken over by the commercial media. Some instances appear to try to escape from that assimilation but end by occupying a narrow band between the sentimental and the jejunely aggressive.

The attention here is on those pop songs which are plainly made by the market for the market. Something escapes, of course, some songs written away from all the market's pressures; and some of those are gifted. But there are not and cannot be a sufficient number of them to meet the weekly needs of the market. A great many are produced routinely and so are industrial products, like much fast food and, as the products of Tin Pan Alley used to be, imitative, stereotyped, formulaic. Then they are closely wrapped in hyperbole which suggests that they are better than, other than, they are. Such objects are certainly not 'good of their kind'. That some may for a week or two rise quite high in the charts is more than anything a success for marketing and also a comment on how easily many young people are caught in peer-group fashions as those are manipulated by that market. The equally formulaic annual effusions are the songs put together – 'crafted' would be too distinguished a word – for the Eurovision Song Contest's somewhat older audiences; there the phenomenon touches rock bottom.

The Cult of Youth is inextricably interwoven with but outlived by that of the celebrities; when youth has gone interest in the newer kind of celebrity takes over, again through the medium of magazines such as *Hello, O.K.* and later publications of their kind. The transition is almost seamless. The Cult of Youth is thus one of the most recognizable and powerful forms of head-counting populism.

The origins are obvious; as so often, they lie in the prospect of profit, in this instance to be found in that newly acquired spare money at virtually all levels of age; and, again not surprisingly; indeed for clear historic reasons, the availability of free money is especially strong among those young people whose parents were unmistakably working-class.

The historic reasons have their roots in working-class life of the old kind, up to about the 1960s. Before then or thereabouts few working-class families had much to spare at the end of each week. But the tradition was that, in the period between leaving school and settling to married life: 'you have a right to have a good time'; 'after all, you're only young once'; there'll be a lot less free time when you have to look after your husband or wife, to bring up the kids, to worry about money, the rent or the mortgage, to spend virtually all your nights in the house ('Thank God for the telly') after what may have been a boring job all day. Most parents will understand if you kick over the traces in the period before all that, and if they can will let you keep quite a lot of your wages; or if, as is common, they do not assume that they have any claim at all on your wages or a substantial part of them.

Today, that free cash starts to flow quite early. A poll in 2001 reported that the average weekly pocket-money of fourteen year olds was thirteen pounds. Even allowing for inflation, that seems a lot; and well worth prizing out of their pockets. Another survey in the same year found that a substantial proportion of seventeen to twenty-four year olds really believe that their idols – in football, pop music and other forms of celebrity – really do consume, use, wear the goods they promote. That is even more surprising, and depressing, than the findings on the size of pocket-money.

That commercial pop music is fed by the pressures of the peer group is predictable. Those pressures too are of course traditional, a historic part of growing up in almost any society, irresistible rites of passage. It is just as predictable in the mass society that those rites will be seized upon, packaged, promoted, expanded, if possible made irresistible. To try to resist that would, except for the congenitally lonely or strong and independently minded, be like ordering the tide to reverse itself. Obviously for many, perhaps for a great majority, it gives their first sense of pleasure at knowing they are going the way their new world is going; that that way may well be emotionally quite different from the world of parents and home; group pleasures take over. This is the age of copying – music, clothes, drinking, holidays, drugs – following, apeing, trend-following, trying things out, being swept along, finding an identity which may come from being with the crowd. Hedonist would be too big and heavy a word to describe this complex run of motives. Back-packing, VSO and the like are too sophisticated and self-aware for all but a small minority; and the pressures in the other direction are insistent.

It would seem to almost all of them irredeemably old-fashioned, beside the point, from another world, to criticize anything in this total and all-embracing culture. Yet listen to and watch a few minutes of, for instance, the BBC's 'Top of the Pops', and notice how calculatedly a kind of group hysteria is created by the insistent excessive sounds, the whirling lights, the invitations from the organizers and prompters on the floor to a kind of abandon which is thumping out all the time; that this freneticism – imposed, invented, beyond any response the participants would have created for themselves – is presented as the only possible way to have a good time. For a slightly more 'adult' audience 'Top of the Pops' was partnered by *The Chair*, which had a similarly synthetic, souped-up frenzy. Such atmospheres have been, have had to be if audience figures are to be maintained, exaggerated over the years. One recent example is the increase in the number of deliberately violent and obscene pop groups. The result is like spiked beer, a mood-enhancer from outside. These things have no social roots; they are moving out to new boundaries as quickly as the struggle between profit and public legislation will allow them.

All this is part of successful membership of the persuasive society. But it is not a pretty sight, in the early twenty-first century and in the most 'advanced' societies of the world. And, yes, most shed it, have to shed it, as real 'reality' takes over on marriage. In the interim, though, there has been a waste of money and time and of the chances of imaginative opening-up; and that is a loss; the world is so much wider and more interesting than any thing the commercial pop world dares suggest. To seek to soften these obvious truths is not a kindness; it is a patronage rather, a thoughtless marking-down masquerading, often unconsciously, as a big-hearted acceptance. That old working-class tag quoted a little earlier – 'You're only young once' – had its main roots in harsh later prospects. It should not be brought in to excuse today's coarse exploitations.

It is extremely important also to be clear just what is being criticized in, for instance, pop (not necessarily 'popular') music. That does not include jazz, jazz musicians and jazz singers such as Ella Fitzgerald, Billy Holliday, Louis Armstrong; or popular singers such as Clarence Frogman Henry, Fats Waller, Nat King Cole and many others. Nor does it refer to the best of Country and Western songs and singers, such as Patsy Cline. The songs in many stage and screen musicals, especially American, are not criticized here; nor are the best of other popular songs and singers, from the Beatles onwards.

In all this, 'youth' has become an unpleasant package-word, to be avoided by journalists of good intent. There are other words, most of them rather staid; but that's all right. 'Youth' is, has to be, identified and approached as a mass with reachable mass tastes, undifferentiated except by their common membership of a particular span of age. The persuaders of 'youth' in the mass society desperately need that audience, not only for obvious profit now but as their trainee-customers for the future. It is becoming clear that in that second stage, when 'real life' in the shape of the pressing but not always unhappy demands of work, family and endless calculations about expenses, may press heavily and most of the time, the persuaders will become for very many irrelevant, powerless, now beside the point. Yet they will go on doing their determined best to continue the endless invitations, suitably modified, or they will begin to direct them to the children of those households; and sometimes they will succeed

This whole catalogue and scenario which embrace so many young people are known to some older people, of course; they are not sufficiently well-known to many others in many parts of society; or, if known, there are handy excuses, mitigations, against recognizing their effects. As I write, Radio 4 has just finished a discussion on why so many adolescents, especially those from sixteen to seventeen, show no interest in politics. Those speakers ('experts') in the studio and those who phoned in ran round the usual track. Most of the blame fell on the politicians and their failings to communicate, or (a circular or self-fulfilling argument) to choose subjects which interested young people. Not one invoked the sort of argument in the last few pages here: that a massive industry addresses just that group – or say, sixteen to twenty-four – intent on amusing the money from their pockets. To the pseudo-world they create, being young and having fun, going with the crowd, are all-embracing; there is no room for politics. Most have had a poor education: we need remember here the figures for inadequate literacy and will not be surprised that most are ignorant about the Second World War, the Holocaust, the European Union. It is easy and probably accurate to reply that, if another war should occur, these young people would respond as well as earlier generations did. That may be true but does not remove the need to look at the ways they are being persuaded to spend their time now, or how that may influence them later in life. It will not be easy to coax many at this time away from all they are being swept along by. Thinking about it begins by recognizing its existence and its power. No discussion about the lack of political interest at that period of life will have any hold on the issue if it does not put right at the forefront this huge and continuous influence. None of this was mentioned in the Radio 4 discussion. Naturally, many young people and the persuaders themselves will be dismissive, even angry, about this criticism of what they will claim as simply the freely-chosen and understandable ways in which young people amuse themselves.

A curious but, one supposes, entirely to be expected result is the way most newspapers have 'jumped on the youth bandwagon'. In the tabloids that is not surprising and needs no explaining. More interesting is the way some of the broadsheets have taken up the cause; are besotted by it. That is not too strong a word; it covers both the commercial need and the little considered enthusiasm. In particular, page after page of their daily and weekly supplements are devoted to all aspects of adolescent taste; not merely pop music and its groups, fashions and films, but the worries of sex and many another teenage concerns. These latter may of course be helpful, but they take their place in even more pages given to the purchasing pleasures of youth, and the surrounding advertisements enforce the general impression. It is all the usual rollercoaster which constantly acquires and then discards the latest, the newest, as it whirls around.

Young people have their needs and rights and deserve space even in the weightiest newspaper. Perhaps the editors or at least their sales managers would also justify it all on the grounds that adolescents become adults and that if they are caught young and learn to like the format they are more likely to be retained. That is another form of the 'catch them young' motto of the cruder persuaders. But at this length and in this thoroughly flimsy manner? One can only conclude that those responsible for these considerable changes have simply not thought enough and better about the nature and implications of the dominant 'youth culture'; as a result they can remain 'relaxed' (a favourite excuse-word); easy-going, compliant; and avoid more nagging revelations; least of all any which might become judgemental.

It is ironic that this shift, and it is a noticeable shift in almost all the broadsheets, has gained its force just at the time when we are being constantly told that the proportion of elderly people in the population is increasing and with it their political importance and buying power. By contrast with the attention given to youth, that to older people is surprisingly muted. The 'heavies', especially in their Sunday supplements, prefer the mixture: 'Youth, along with or with the promise of executive-style living in suitable homes, and meals in the latest fashionable restaurants.' A strange mixture except that, on closer examination, their youth sections are heavily slanted towards adolescent budding-executives (though nestling in the small coloured advertisements at the back are a few for electric stair-lifts). Add the proliferation of nightclubs of various kinds and different class-affiliations but all linked by heat, noise, drink and drugs. Is this the best that the advanced societies can do for their successful young people? And lap-dancing for older men.

Two snapshots to end this section. A Farnham (population about 30,000) taxi-driver spent his time on a fairly long journey grumbling that the town was dead. His ten daughters could find nothing to amuse them. There are many pubs in the town, some focusing on attracting teenagers, but those were not mentioned. There are discos and nightclubs in Aldershot and Guildford, each only a few miles away, but that can be expensive for those not already in work. Unless the mother worked also, the parents could hardly afford to give each of those ten girls anything approaching that average thirteen pounds a week in pocket-money which most fourteen year olds apparently have. There is no cinema now in Farnham; and the Film Society, of the usual kind, would probably put them off socially. There are mutliplex cinemas at Aldershot and Guildford.

Farnham has well over a hundred voluntary societies, as have most towns of a similar size; they cater for all ages and many types of interest; there is a very good sports complex whose core is the large swimming pool. That has spawned all the usual sporting clubs. There is a welcoming but not particularly well-funded public library. The countryside around is lovely; walking, cycling and other outdoor clubs open that to their members.

But the taxi-driver insisted that Farnham is 'a dead-beat town', one which offered nothing to young people. In fact it can cater for a very wide range of interests so long as those interests do not wholly focus themselves on clubbing on the spot, rather than a few miles away, and the like. Apparently, the taxi-driver's daughters had not been offered, by their school, home or immediate peer-group, the prospect of any hinterland beyond that narrow focus. Nor did the driver himself seem to look beyond nightly television; there was no mention of gardening, or an allotment, or any hobby inside or outside the home; or of the pub, come to that, which could be a good sign. Of two other taxi-drivers I came to know, one was a keen gardener, the other a breeder of prize-winning canaries.

Fifty years ago, when I drew a somewhat similar picture of the leisure time of some young people in a small Yorkshire town, it was criticized as too depressing. The criticism was a reflex action by people who did not want to hear of or make such judgements. It stands today, only the exploitation has become more intense and effective.

Second picture: two young graduates living at present in part-nership. They had just toured in the Far East, comfortably, not back-packing; they were happy and agreeable, very pleasant to meet. They could afford an expensive holiday since each was, only a few years after graduation, earning 'good money'. She was a chemist in a firm producing heavily promoted downmarket cosmetics; he was a sales executive (salesman; commercial trav-eller) in a firm making chemically enhanced 'tasty' snacks, also heavily promoted especially in pubs and clubs. One cannot claim that either of those jobs was criminal, but considering that the efforts of both firms were to persuade people to buy frivolous, expensive and probably unhealthy products, the word 'immoral' would not be altogether out of place.

Those young people are likely to go on, unaware that there is anything to be said against their choice of occupation, and its relevance to the expense of giving them university degrees. They will probably live a blameless life in the usual senses, professional middle-class, neighbourly, perhaps with some voluntary work for the community; they will continue to have their expensive holidays, at least until children arrive; later, there may be golf or bridge or gardening, and television. They may even vote Labour or Liberal Democrat and perhaps read the *Guardian* or the *Independent*. They will become steady consumers; apart from the voluntary activities, they will not think much about issues outside their well-heeled lives. They are and will remain typical products of the commercial, commodity-mad, and unthinkingly prosperous West.

Chapter 5

Broadcasting Yesterday and Today, Chiefly by the BBC

'To apply it [broadcasting] to the dissemination of the shoddy, the vulgar and the sensational would be a blasphemy against human nature.'

(Lord Reith, *Broadcast over Britain*)

The Public Service Principle and Independence

One can almost hear the light-headed laughter at Lord Reith's use of the vocabulary of the kirk, especially in the use of that word 'blasphemy'. But his prose is not as simple and uncomplicated as it might at first seem. He does not stop at that word or add what could then be implied; 'blasphemy against God'; he makes the argument secular by adding, instead: 'against human nature'. For that, he might have substituted 'blasphemy against democracy', which is also true though less powerful. His chosen form is more deeply rooted, is against what is due – ethically, it must imply – to 'human nature'. In the light of Reith's assertion, the counter-arguments of those who dismiss his definition of what broadcasting is and should do as out-of-date, because almost eighty years old, are revealed as puerile. He is writing from within the assurance that broadcasting should be founded on the principles of public service. That is no more out-of-date than *habeas corpus* or trial by jury; and is as essential as those are

108

to a democracy's proper working. Reith's marmorial style is in all important respects up-to-date.

The public service principle is even more up-to-date in its universality than what may be thought to guide the press. The press, whether responsible or irresponsible, reaches self-selected audiences and so, in most of its forms and titles, tends to feed the beliefs, opinions and often prejudices of each of those audiences. Where it does more than that it too may rise above itself and move towards a democratic, a public, service. By contrast broadcasting is in its nature, and potentially if not always actually, able to reach all of us at any place, age, time and disposition. It is therefore the most powerful organ, if we so wish, that any would-be democracy can have (and a totalitarian society, of course, which uses those qualities for its own ends). But democratic broadcasting is free: it can tell things as they are or lie about them; it can amuse and in that more than in most of its other activities may bring all parts of society together in a shared sense of what is funny; or it can seek to produce laughter ignominiously. It can take us by surprise by revealing that the world is wider than we are used to thinking and its problems not to be lightly approached, but well worth facing squarely.

It, especially television, to which I shall give most attention, is revelatory. It can offer sudden flashes of insight in pictures or words; epiphanies, which we do not forget. My own store includes a big beer-bellied man in a working-men's club saying he felt no responsibility if he made a girl pregnant: 'That's her fucking look-out.' That captured something of the essence of a horrible subculture. Then an early middle-aged woman talking quietly and with no smugness about how rewarding it had been to foster children with special needs. That was goodness unobtrusively revealed. And, in a programme about *au pairs,* there was a youngish woman talking with hard confidence about what she required of those young women, and exuding all the time a deeply uncharitable personality, so that you knew that no young woman would be well-treated there. That speaker too was of course unconscious of the awful impression she was making. So was her sister spirit, a hotel owner who, interviewed during the foot and mouth crisis, could only rage intemperately at the government.

Other epiphanies are snapshots: President Nixon getting out of his limousine at Notre Dame in Paris and suddenly half-ducking back because he had realized that his security men were not in position; Bevin when Foreign Secretary also getting out if his car and moving off, paying no attention to his wife who was still in the car; presumably he was totally preoccupied. Finally Duncan Sandys, when Commonwealth Secretary, coming down the steps of an aircraft at Heathrow to be met by a group of reporters. No doubt he was tired and pressed; but he was inexcusably rude and brushed them off as if he were an irascible squire rebuking his irritating workmen. That deserved a place in the reports of those journalists; but most are inured to rolling with the blows on such occasions.

Epiphanies are different from deliberate revelations, being unplanned, accidental; planned revelatory programmes are deliberate exposures of the corrupt habits of plumbers, double-glazing salesmen, loan-sharks and many another. They are very common nowadays and very useful; it is a rich seam.

Back to the main line. For all the self-flattery about their capacity for resolute action, the British tend to prefer slow-moving, even phlegmatic, local, family and neighbourhood-centred society, and that has its virtues; it discourages ricocheting from one apparently magical social prescription to another. Yet occasionally, recalling Isaiah Berlin's hedgehog and fox, we have a particularly good idea at the same time as a willingness to apply it: as in many nineteenth-century reforms, including the cultural. That is shown in the growth of public education, the creation of public libraries, public parks and allotments. In the past century one fine example is the founding of the National Health Service in its original form, the expansion of higher education, and the institution of the Open University.

The most original and inspired socio/cultural idea of the twentieth century was to require this immensely powerful new instrument, broadcasting, to have public service at its heart. To that basic notion it added, with classic simplicity, force and comprehensiveness, the main constituents which emerge from that idea. British broadcasting must 'inform, educate and entertain'. No other prescription could be more deceptively simple and apparently easy to swallow? But it has sharp teeth, beginning in the hidden but inescapable assumption: that all those objects must be pursued honestly, so far as possible objectively, not for hidden or overt persuasion of any kind, political or commercial, but for the public good. It is no wonder that some in many countries sought to follow that example; or looked back longingly at it when their hopes failed.

To pursue this central, disinterested, path will never be easy. But consider the alternatives, or a mixture of them. The limitations of broadcasting under direct governmental control are evident in all parts of the world; it becomes a political tool and so loses its potential power to inform and educate impartially; and entertainment becomes either puritanically limited by the vision of the politicians, or a safe bromide of a dish with no comical or satirical spice.

The BBC has given over the years several outstanding and direct examples of the value of separation from direct governmental control and of the courage needed to exercise it. As when, in the autumn of 1956 the Prime Minister, Anthony Eden, tried to make the BBC the mouthpiece of the government's position on the Suez operation. That was not the position of the House of Commons; the opposition opposed the enterprise. The BBC Governors refused to become the instrument of government propaganda, even though threatened with a governmental takeover. They were to some extent protected by their status as a body created by Royal Charter rather than by Act of Parliament, but defiance of that sort is never easy.

The problem was to a lesser degree repeated during the Falkands expedition, when some MPs took exception to what they foolishly and mistakenly thought was unpatriotic language in certain BBC broadcasts about the engagements. Those MPs and Peers called the BBC's chairman and director general to a meeting where they were harangued about patriotism; which both rightly thought unnecessary and discreditable.

On such occasions the BBC does walk on a very thin line. It is not the creature of any one government, but some MPs of whatever political party think it should be. Some also think the BBC should mirror the conventionally-assumed status quo, as in 'Thought for the Day' and, trickier, its attitude to Royalty and Royal occasions.

Broadcasting financed by advertising is hardly better than when under political control. The balance sheet between the broadcasters and the advertisers has to be governed by simple listener-or-viewer count; except in those niche areas where the buying power of a sizeable minority justifies payment for selective advertising. The dead weight of the search for the largest audience at peak times and as often as possible outside those – however much the concerned if residual attempt to live up to the public service remit may nag at some – that search more and more determines that populist programming wins, programmes which do not disturb or suggest wider horizons, which offer instant and repetitive gratifications, whose world is, except inter-mittently, closed to other considerations.

This sort of argument must seem almost incredible to very many in Britain at the turn of the new century. The majority of viewers now assume what Americans have long assumed: that the overwhelming function of television is to provide entertainment; much of it paid for by advertisements.

Some things sometimes escape, of course: a writer offers a programme outside the formulaic and a producer, remembering the public service idea and marshalling his creative professionalism, manages to recreate that on the screen; but inevitably such moments have to be rare; and are becoming rarer.

Some people argue that television in the USA invalidates this argument, because it can produce splendid programmes which owe their making to the responsible public conscience or the inventive comic ability of broadcasters rather than repeating what is already known to satisfy the market. This is partially true. And some of those programmes (such as 'The Simpsons', 'The Sopranos' and others) straddle the two. Those are fine flowers in the dust-heap; the USA is big enough, wealthy enough and diverse enough to allow both kinds of programmes to appear, but one kind – the populist – is enormously more the norm than the other. And must be financially dominant or the other kind could not be afforded. In general, American television addresses massed or compartmentalized audiences; which is why you rarely hear it discussed in groups of highly educated people over there, and then the talk is usually dismissive. There is, of course, much talk in college departments of Media Studies, but most of those pay little attention to the socio-political background; and when they do it is taken as given. The chairman of the USA's regulatory body once described American television as 'a vast wasteland'; that judgement is still substantially true, when you think of what might be.

Both alternatives – governmental control and advertising revenue tied directly to the production of programmes – do not encourage wide and good programming. The dangers of governmental control are obvious and were noted earlier. The link at the commercial boardroom level between the making of programmes and the increase in advertising revenue can be fatal. Television is then by its nature harassed, unwilling to cast its bread on the waters, to widen and vary range; because it cannot easily wait for types of programme to mature. If there is near-adequate legislation, as here, the patient does not die but suffers a disabled existence. At bottom, it is always pushing towards the production of skewed, un-public service, results. No form of creative activity can do its work properly if it is either ruled by fear or by profit-seeking; fear of government intervention or, worse in the long but less evident run, by the shareholders' never-ending drive for greater profit. That takes the eye off the making of good programmes on to the making of programmes which will produce the largest number of listeners or viewers for the longest span of time.

The two are only occasionally compatible. Professionally proud programme makers cannot at the same time serve two masters without becoming cross-eyed. They should be free to make *good* programmes in a not-primarily-head-counting sense; they should not ignore or scorn possible audiences; indeed, they would be delighted if they attracted a large audience; but not at the expense of what they are trying to say, not at the cost of intellectual honesty or imaginative creativity. They will never say: 'That kind of programme [perhaps made by competitors] got a very big audience. What's the formula? How can I repeat it?' As public service broadcasters they will make mistakes about pro-ductions or audiences; that will be their difficulty and their freedom. As makers of programmes with an eye overwhelmingly on audience size related to class and cash considerations they will be the creatures of the advertisers who pay them; and they are not interested in the complex nature of *good* broadcasting; they are interested solely in what broadcasts have the best results, in numbers and socio-economic relevance to their targets. All too obviously that is not the same as an interest in open-approached broadcasting, and least of all in broadcasting in the public interest.

As we shall have to say more than once, 'the public interest' is not the same as, nor does it greatly overlap with, 'what interests the public'. The first is an altogether wider and deeper thing;

and so more complex, as are all three of its stated elements, even the duty to 'entertain'. They go to the roots of a society's conversation with itself, rather than being concerned most of the time with tickling their audiences tummies for the greater profit of a few. That some people have in the last decades been willing to try entirely to discard public service principles if they can get away with the practice is not surprising and recalls Shakespeare's 'base Indian', who threw a pearl away.

There must be some legislation of broadcasting, and there is in almost all countries. Some legislators are virtually toothless, as in the USA; others are government stooges, operators of punitive censorship; as in many a one-party state. British legislation is neither altogether toothless nor punitive. Naturally, it says for a start: 'Thou shalt not'; here its approach is generally like that applied to print. It says: thou shalt not be obscene nor racist nor libellous; all obvious warnings.

It differs from most other forms of legislation in that it also says: 'Thou shalt'. It is positive about what broadcasting should do; it points to open doors. Having corralled a narrow range of forbidden practices, it goes on to encourage broadcasters to move out, to act positively. It says: 'inform, educate and entertain', in that brief but adequate invitation to take off, to experiment, to be free. It lays more stress on liberation than on restriction. The original Independent Broadcasting Authority's code included 'Thou shalts' also. The 1990 (Thatcher) Broadcasting Act relieved the commercial companies of those duties. They immediately dropped such programmes; which were not likely to attract audiences of the size and composition the advertisers liked.

In between there is an injunction which straddles both sides of the issue, that on 'balance', which looks simple but is harder than most to live up to, as broadcasters have constantly found. It straddles both sides because it contains another restricting injunction: 'thou shalt not be partisan', but expresses it as a positive: 'thou

115

shalt be balanced'. Between the two there can be nightmares of interpretation. One person's balance is another's bias. Another person's balance is a wishy-washy form of: 'on the one hand, on the other', which can leave the listener or viewer dangling in uncertainties about what is really being said. Huw Wheldon of the BBC used often to give brilliant interpretations on the run. When rightly exasperated with objectors who demanded balance within every programme, which could emasculate them, he suggested that balance – in major issues whether political or social – should be assessed over a year's output of relevant programmes. Some MPs would resist that – strongly.

It may be apt to bring in here another of Wheldon's favourite declarations: that one of the public service broadcaster's main aims should be: 'To make good programmes popular and popular programmes good.' That can sound pawky or superior or self-evident. It can also be interpreted as much more weighty and percipient. By 'good' programmes he meant those made because the broadcaster thought them, though perhaps 'difficult', of great value and wished without 'selling them' by over simplification to make them widely available. By popular programmes he meant those unlikely to appeal to and not designed specifically for a highly educated audience but which became 'good' because they too did not sell out by patronising, or secretly despising, their audience's taste, by talking down to them. Of the first type the best instances might be much on Radio 4 and, on television, some programmes on history, the universe and the arts. Of the second type one is almost spoilt for choice, from 'The Goon Show' to 'The Fast Show', via 'Hancock's Half Hour', 'Morecambe and Wise', 'Steptoe and Son', 'Till Death us do Part', 'Yes, Minister', 'Dad's Army', 'Fawlty Towers', 'One Foot in the Grave', 'The Office', 'The Royle Family', 'The League of Gentlemen' and beyond. Programmes such as those helped to show that in the possession of a funny bone, Britain was virtually classless; and that is a major discovery.

But that word 'classless' is not accurate there. 'Across classes' would be right as a description of the audience. Most of the programmes exploit, get much of their humour from, the sense of class itself and its convolutions; we recognize it and laugh at it, as a kind of release. By contrast, today's 'Comedy Night' seems to think that to insert 'fuck' two or three times in each sentence is the height of humour.

Wheldon's vision was truly democratic. In that, he was unlike the just as sincere first Director General of the Independent Television Authority. He, when challenged about some of the low-level programmes commercial programme put out in its first five years (until they were advised not to let the pursuit of greater profits lead them down that muddy path), replied: 'Ah but, you see, I do not despise the pursuits of ordinary people', without, apparently, being able to see that that sententious remark could conceal its own low opinion of 'ordinary folk', which is itself not very far from unconsciously despising their pursuits and them. He happened to be from the Antipodes but that has no significance, except that it probably explained his distaste for the British sense of class divisions and his defence of 'ordinary people'. A similar, this time self-congratulatory, utterance was made by an Oxford Philosophy don at about the same time. He was defending in thin air programmes he admittedly never watched.

Wheldon's epigrams were always based on a firm belief in the public service idea and its widest and best implications. At its best, British broadcasting has lived up to those implications; and that can sometimes include, against the odds and though their owners' obedience to the public service idea is often lip-service forced upon them against their nature, even the two main commercial television channels.

The result of, above all, regulation which not only forbade some things but positively encouraged others which embodied the public service idea, was the establishment of a broadcasting system which has been admired, especially by broadcasters themselves, across the world. Admired and trusted above all for trying to tell the truth, not to put out government propaganda. The BBC World Service surpassed itself in this throughout the Second World War, as even the German authorities knew. Earlier, John Reith and his cohorts of mainly Oxbridge men (and some women) were often and justly mocked for their starchy ways. But they had hold of important truths about the possibilities of broadcasting; they have by now given way to much more widely recruited colleagues, which is as it should be. But the times do not now encourage staff to ponder on the interpretation and application for the present-day of public service principles. Yet to some extent the model holds. It was right, if a little surprising, that a top executive in the commercial television sector, well aware of the contradictory pressures under which he worked and not mealy-mouthed, said: 'The BBC keeps us all honest.'

One now retired from the BBC's higher echelons said, as he looked at those conflicting drives particularly in the commercial area and at the existing restraints within broadcasting's regulations, that if those checks were removed the pressure to have public executions would at once begin, and they would have the largest conceivable audiences. When he first said that, it seemed incredible, especially in the light of the rejection of capital punishment by Parliament, if not by a majority of the population. Some decades on, it seems less unlikely; and may well begin in the USA. It came uncomfortably near in the arguments there about the execution of the Oklahoma bomber. Profits, more than creative or 'democratic' impulses, are always trying to push out the boundaries; on the grounds of course that this-or-that is 'What the public want'. It is the burden of this chapter that what 'the public – we – want' should not be a first or overriding aim. There are better criteria.

The Licence Fee and the Treasury

Inextricably connected to the idea of broadcasting free from political or commercial pressures is the institution of the licence fee. By some who certainly should know better, including many politicians (naturally including those who see profit for themselves in that abolition), it is reviled as 'a regressive poll tax'; a favoured phrase which rolls impressively off the tongue but means no more than that it applies to all without distinction of means or any other criteria. It is not entirely true and in recent years has become even less true, as more exemptions are made. But the decision that it should exist at all and that it should then apply to almost all households, is central to the British conception of good broadcasting; in this it is rather like the principle that a dog licence should cost us all the same; or that it should cost us no more to send a letter to the Outer Hebrides than to the nearest borough (though that principle is already looking shaky).

We have noted the risks of funding by advertising. Could there be safe, hassle-free, ring-fenced, payment by government rather like the National Health Service; and with protections against those risks of political interference noted earlier? No, because the two institutions are different. The National Health Service raises plenty of political questions but the reporting and analysis of day-by-day politics is not one of its central purposes, as it is of the broadcasters. Because of that and its powerful implications, and for other reasons, the BBC must be firmly protected from political pressures. The licence fee is, in that, a central strut of the public service idea.

Naturally, governments like to get their hands on the money thus pulled in and to decide where it goes. So a senior Treasury official was able to pronounce to a Committee of Inquiry that a direct link, assumed by almost all licence fee payers, between what the public paid and the broadcasters' making of programmes, did not exist. To the Treasury, the licence fee was 'a licence to operate a radio and/or television receiver', much like a car or dog licence; it was not a payment to receive programmes.

Quite separately, he argued, the Treasury gave the BBC money, after due discussion, for its programme-making. So, no link with the licence fee? 'No.' And you have over the years given the BBC much less than you have received in licence fees? 'Yes?' Have you ever given the BBC more than you had received in licence fees; that surely is a fair concomitant? '[With a smile] Oh no.' But you could? 'Theoretically, perhaps.' You realize that most people assume a direct link between the licence fee and the BBC's provision for making programmes? 'Yes. It exists, it is a mistaken hypothesis.' Perhaps, his listeners felt as he ended, that they might call it a Platonic definition of the relations between licence fee income and Treasury disbursements.

Nevertheless, the fact that the licence fee exists and that the BBC operates under a Royal Charter have, taken together, saved it from many depredations; especially from some MPs who do not quite understand the protective force of the two elements. Such invasions have become more common and insistent since the end of the 1970s.

Those who would like to be rid of the licence fee are fond of quoting market research which seems to show that most people would prefer not to pay it. If you ask a restricted question you will have a restricted answer. But if you point out what the licence fee ensures in the enormous range and variety of both BBC Radio and BBC Television (as contrasted with the relatively limited breadth of the commercial provision), a range and variety that commercial drives would not encourage, even if they were the sole providers; if you add a comparison of prices between, let us say, the most limited of Sky's packages with what you receive for less money from the licence fee, then people see at once what a remarkable bargain the licence fee is. Add to that an imponderable which nevertheless is held by and influences a great many people. That is, a sense of respect for the BBC, a feeling that it stands for something nationally as few other broadcasting systems do or can. Which is different from a feeling that the broadcasters are simply the mouthpiece of government; but rather that in spite of its occasional stuffinesses the BBC is trusted to try to be objective, not to be any government's or commercial concern's mouthpiece; and to treat big occasions adequately. That is why it is still turned to on those big occasions, especially at moments of national concern; this as a matter of informed habit.

The history of the BBC is more complex than that of most large institutions. It is an integral part of the country's cultural (in the wide sense) history, of what has been happily called its 'quarrels with itself' and of its moments at peace with itself. It can reveal the adequacy or inadequacy of those quarrels with itself, our reactions to social changes and political pressures. It throws a unique light on many of the themes discussed in these pages. Incidentally, more than most large institutions, it reveals the power of certain individuals (John Reith, Hugh Carleton-Greene, John Birt), a power like that of someone controlling a huge ship, causing it to turnabout, so as to make what they judge to be the right response to climate changes. The BBC has been – is – both a mirror and a compass. To do these things, to adopt this unwritten and often unperceived role, it has had to honour the principles of public service; and this has required what one who served the corporation for many years described as 'a degree of unselfishness' in its staff, the willingness to work for less money than was on offer elsewhere and to resist the temptation to make programmes which fed their egos rather than illuminated their subjects. The same person, viewing decline in the quality of many BBC programmes, asks: 'Could it be that at a time of technological scarcity we operated at a level above public taste?' The answer is probably that, in the light of their public service commitment and all that implied about respecting democracy and its citizens, they did sometimes to some extent aim above many people's heads. That is better than aiming below the navel. The right balance is extremely tricky; there is little doubt that today broadcasters, still quoting their democratic duty, sometimes and increasingly aim below public taste. An executive in commercial television, formerly at the BBC, complained that far from finding a benchmark in the BBC, the corporation was forgetting its duty towards public service, was often encroaching on what he thought of as the commercial channels' ground, and beating them on it. Which is rather like a loose woman complaining that formerly respectable housewives, far from setting a good example, were amateurs moving on to her pitch. Or 'Why don't you set us a fine example and so help too to keep us virtuous?'

Achievements, Sometimes Against the Odds

Before going further with what will be largely criticism of the BBC it will be fair to recall its, and sometimes the commercial arm's, achievements. Of course the BBC has produced in both sound and vision some splendid programmes of high intellectual and imaginative standard. It did so from the beginning. Yet in what it thought of as its more 'popular' (the word was often rather weaselly used) programmes in the early days it often sounded rather like a product of Oxbridge bending to amuse the masses. Television did not fully enter until after the Second World War and is by its nature a more open instrument. But the change had occurred before then and is largely attributable to that war. Radio programmes designed to keep 'the workers happy' at their work began in very much the old style. The break-through, and it was characteristic of the English temper, came with comedy, typified by ITMA. There is a direct line from that to those later comedy programmes.

Since then we have owed much to television. We have had first-class historical, scientific, technological, natural history, sport, D.I.Y. and other programmes of all kinds. We have had admirable news gathering and analyses of current affairs at home and abroad (especially in the Third World); and arts programmes, also of many kinds and at many levels. From the same sources have come that series of unparalleled comic programmes whose audiences often cut across differences in age, social class, and educational training. This is the briefest general resume of a monumental achievement; which is widely under-rated or unacknowledged. We shall see later that sometimes it now lists heavily so as to beat the competition; so that one wonders whether public service has been overtaken by 'show biz'.

Recognition of the record has been weakened by today's less impressive practice, culturally rather than technically. The BBC itself is slow to recognize the change, since any large organisation appoints the people suitable for its current practice; hence many of today's broadcasters neither know nor care much for the public service idea; if they are reminded of it, their relativist post-modernism (if that is not a too grandiose phrase for their background and approach) takes over and dismisses the entire argument.

If you accuse them of producing too much rubbish, they either do not recognize the judgement, or any of that kind – or they point to the comparatively side-lined 'posh', 'highbrow', or simply genuine and serious programmes they still produce. This is the *Boule de Suif* argument in reverse; the aristocrats get the prostitutes out of a hole; or it sounds like giving a genteel tea-party to a few old ladies to fend off criticism of their mugging by the mob. BBC4 introduces itself with the self-righteous: 'Every-body needs a place to think' which, translated, means 'here's your smart ghetto'. That toe-curling sentence sets in place even more firmly an undesirable social division. Compartmentalism of that sort is manifestly undemocratic, and is what we have called earlier consigning the bulk of the population to the carousel, the level, valueless carousel.

In defence, there are always disguising words available. 'Diversity' is a favourite with spokesmen of both commercial television and the BBC, to justify the current shaming broth. It is used to validate providing much rubbish for 'the masses' with a small mixture of 'serious, highbrow, arty' programmes meant to buy off regulators and critics.

So, again, organizations recruit the people they need to sustain and advance their purposes as they interpret them. Or by the half-hidden weight of the current BBC 'philosophy', they condition existing staff or under-educated newcomers. Today's defenders of the BBC's performance, most being appointed according to that rule, will either not understand the counter-arguments, or not accept them, and provide for themselves an acceptable reinterpretation. Faced with such instances one is reminded of Sir John Harington's pithy couplet of four hundred years ago. It was aimed at the nature of governments but applies just as well, if melodramatically, here: 'Treason doth never prosper, what's the reason?/For if it prosper, none dare call it treason.' We reinvent our aims and language to fit the day.

That is to be expected. It is more of a surprise to see how many of the 'intelligentsia', or simply of highly educated people, do not have this critical perspective at all but happily confine themselves to the programmes they recognize as made for them; or for a change they practise a little cultural slumming and say how much they enjoy a programme they readily admit is 'trash' (such as 'Big Brother' or the tackily frenetic presentations around the mid-week and Saturday announcements of Lottery results); or they do not recognize at all the case against a programme which they enjoy in just the way devised and intended by the makers, who are then aiming not only at 'the bottom end of the market', but also and from knowledge at the genteel middle-brow level; as when an Oxbridge don 'confesses' to being a fan of that cherry-picking, savoury tit-bits, repetitive anthology of classical music which slides down easily: Classic FM. Oxbridge dons tend to pop up often in such would-be lowbrow roles.

One need not be unaware of or unsympathetic towards the BBC's difficulties, or fail to understand their fears, as in: 'If we lost too much of the market the justification for the licence fee would be called into question.' But they have there placed themselves at least partially within a false dilemma. Good quality is indivisible and to be sought at all levels, from the 'light' to the 'heavy', from the comical to the serious; it arises there and in all spaces in between from integrity before your subject and respect for your audience. That may sound slightly too grand for the occasion. So let us once again remember Huw Wheldon and his ready apophthegms. He avoided above all the primal sin: thinking of your audience first and only then deciding what will affect them, what will be instantly palatable. That is a recipe for echoes-back of the already accepted, and typically Wheldon used to say something like this: 'One of my best tests about any proposed subject is: "Does it engage me thoroughly and honestly? If so, then it's a fair guess that if I treat it properly the programme which comes out of it will genuinely interest many viewers."' That might not apply in the unlikely event that a producer had a thoroughly trite mind. For others, it is not a bad start, even if a producer's chief love (among many) were stamp collecting. Good producers have either a wide or a deep range of interests, and preferably both; then their enthusiasms can guide the craft and their audiences are likely to be satisfied in a way they may not have expected. Above all, good producers will avoid brain-storming office sessions which try primarily to peer into the minds of the viewers so as to guess and second-guess what might amuse them. Fortunately, many programmes conceived in that way have collapsed; but by no means all, not enough thoroughly to warn off the confidently rubbish-bound producers.

Before setting out to make the specific case that the process of dumbing down has occurred, it may be useful to cast a brief glance at of the condition of some branches of both radio and television, chiefly from the BBC.

The BBC's Radio 4 is generally considered the most successful of their sound channels, in still upholding some of the main features of public service broadcasting. There is much in this claim; it is based on a wide and varied output ranging from, especially, help for disadvantaged individuals and groups to most of the best radio comedy shows, some of which have a large audience mixed by age and class.

Radio 4's variety is admirable, the treatment usually intelligently prepared and well-considered. With some justice it has been called the bulletin board of the middle-classes, though lower-middle classes might be more exact. Its news and current affairs programmes do not usually talk down, being rather sober; and hard-hitting when needed (and sometimes when not – conversely, they can on occasion play softly where one might have expected hard-hitting). Its specifically helpful programmes such as 'You and Yours', money and food programmes and many others make up a tapestry which really does give a picture, though rather staid, of important aspects of everyday English life and interests. It regularly puts out readings from old and new fiction, though usually and unmistakably middle-brow, and still manages to broadcast old and new drama. It spends considerable time and money on many minorities, and has a valuable telephonic helpline which serves them and others. It ties in usefully with the internet. One could go on; the credit column is long.

The more questionable elements in today's Radio 4 derive from typical uncertainties of the time. Its old assurances are no longer available, especially those related to social class and manners of addressing them. This is shown as well as anywhere in their programmes about books. They are usually, as is much in their society, unwilling to make judgements; judgements divide and may make some listeners feel ignorant. If possible, no one should be 'put off', especially by the inclusion of anything which seems 'highbrow'. Book programmes favour presentation-with-discussion and, even if those chosen are not current bestsellers (some may have appeared long ago), they do tend to belong to the middle-range in their intellectual and imaginative demands, and so does the presenting as a whole. If Lawrence's *Women in Love* had been first published today it would have been unlikely to be selected; and as for *Ulysses*! There is little if any suggestion of a bigger and better literary world outside. This limitation is partnered by and reflected in the excessive language of adulation in which most invited speakers seem expected to present their particular choices. After some of those epithets, there would be few left with which to praise Lawrence and Joyce. The poetry programmes are somewhat better but, no doubt led by the same hesitations, tend to mix good poetry with popular versifying. The 'this won't hurt a bit; in fact it's rather nice' effort to avoid embarrassing anyone is pervasive. A mixture of the good and the indifferent doesn't make for a successful introduction; it takes the eye off the best object.

The barn-door rusticism of 'The Archers' is again and again being 'modernized', brought 'up to date' – well, made more melodramatic – especially as to sexual habits, so that one wonders whether more listeners than we hear about are feeling bereft. Or are the editors seeking a younger audience? And finding it? And do the old guard of listeners soldier on whatever horrible things happen in Ambridge?

Most curious of all are those *ad hominem* gestures by which readers are warmly urged to phone in with their views of important and often extremely difficult issues. A democratic forum? Maybe, but it should go without saying that those who write or phone or fax, being self-selected, are not likely to represent the shape or spread of attitudes across the population. In general, opinions are likely to come from the relatively few who congenitally feel moved to 'go public', from the more assertive citizens, the aggressively prejudiced and the nuttily opinionated. Careful winnowing, and I am sure it is tried, may appear to correct that into a kind of balance. But you cannot make a true balance from an inherently unbalanced sample. So there ensues not a true balance, but rather a distribution made by the programmers to ensure that it does not suggest too wild an imbalance than they have already found; it remains artificial.

When the Third Programme began, not long after the war, well-educated people were pleased. Together with each week's issue of 'The Listener', it provided good nourishment for the mind and, for Britain, an exceptionally wide introduction to the best music after those six long years, especially if one was by then working in the outer provinces.

Its early history can seem rather comical now, especially in some of its statements of aims, such as the one which claimed to be seeking to recreate something of the best conversation in universities' senior common rooms. To that some academics responded that in their senior common room the conversation was chiefly about mortgages, family and football. Certainly the records of the channel's management meetings in those early days have an old-fashioned, almost dustily academic, air. But not always; that channel gave Dylan Thomas and many another their early opportunities; there are accounts of penniless poets going along from Fitzrovia to Upper Regent Street confident of a warm greeting and perhaps the offer of a programme or some other kind of help. The Third Programme experimented with new kinds of work unique to its medium. Its music coverage was unashamedly and rightly high-level; it did not talk down; it did do much to increase the appreciation of classical music.

Radio 3 still does some good work, but now more jumpily than when it was born. Once again the old assurance has gone, the fear of being called highbrow and elitist. In a recent conversation on air, the channel controller uttered the usual reductive defence; that no distinction of worth can automatically be made between pop music and Mozart. Each can be excellent *in its own way* and has its place. We are back with Beethoven and the Beatles. From the controller of Radio 3 that sounds ominous.

Jazz has long had its place on the channel and there's an argument for including something of the best in popular music. But from the conversation on that occasion the impression came that many fewer distinctions were being made, that the floodgates to a wide plain were being opened. One can – it has been done here – argue that a mix of types of programme is central to the BBC's purposes, especially to give us all, the listeners and viewers, the chance to see that the world is more varied and interesting than we habitually think. But since there are already four other channels, ranging from one which offers mainly pop music through a resolutely light channel to one heavily concerned with sport (5 Live) to Radio 4. At such a time Radio 3's role as a channel of the intellectual and imaginative life should be reinforced. Yet today light classical and film music are parts of Radio 3's regular output; that is dilution.

The introduction of Channel 4 television was all in all to the good, especially because it severed the disabling knot which ties programme-making to advertising revenue. To anyone who had welcomed the 1962 Pilkington Committee's recommendation of that approach to any new non-BBC channel, it was particularly appreciated. Latterly that knot has been tied and, although Channel 4 is not a profit-making body since it has no shareholders, the temptation to link programme-making decisions to their likely attraction to advertisers is obvious and dangerous. One programme-commissioner planning a new situation comedy asked likely advertisers to view it in the making and comment; until the channel's director, alerted to the invitation, forbade it. The founding fathers must have been horrified.

There was an air of imaginative invention about the initial team as a whole and, also on the whole, it produced some imaginative, including risk-taking, programmes such as that illustrating a long poem by Tony Harrison. There was some brashness, not so much dumbing down as post-modernizing up.

In 2001, the managing director Michael Jackson left for the United States and, inevitably, an even more lucrative appointment. There is no need to imply that it was chiefly the extra money which drew him; it seems just as likely that he wanted a change and a new challenge. He will get that and may well find the atmosphere even more to his taste than Britain was. Or perhaps not. A lecture he gave just before his departure was inadequate to its subject. Its wide social assertions, rooted neither in close observation nor in informed thought, showed no great understanding of British cultural change. Instead, he was content with rattling around a few of the fashionable ideas which help sustain the myths of a new smart 'classless' society. Probably those also helped to suggest and justify certain elements of his approach to programme-making; they were not likely to add to our knowledge of new and illuminating approaches in broadcasting. His successor came from the top echelon's of the BBC; that switch – even after again allowing the need for a change of scene and the attraction of a substantial increase in pay – always seems like, if not a betrayal, then a dereliction.

The successor will inherit some excellent operations, beginning with the news and some in-depth current affairs programmes. He will also meet some of the kind invented specifically for one kind of assumed audience rather than because of the intrinsic interest of the subject; such as the incestuous, cheap, apparently endless chain of compilations usually entitled 'The Twelve Best TV-somethings of the Year'. He will find the falsely-called 'reality' programmes such as 'Big Brother'. For such programmes the title 'reality' does duty for 'cheap self-exposure by rather silly young people seeking publicity at any cost'. *The Economist* rightly called this kind of television humiliation 'one of the tawdriest popular genres'. The new managing director, who has apparently listed 'Big Brother' as among his core, to be kept, programmes, will find some surprisingly silly but would-be flashy programmes, such as those devoted to the music of the millennium. Some of the presenters, to judge from their choices, thought a millennium was a hundred years, the last hundred; and that the whole canon of music was pop or, at its extreme 'high-brow' level, jazz. Did the producers at least know no better? Or were they so totally habituated to populism's lack of historical or intellectual knowledge as to think those two inexcusable foreclosures, given the title of the series, justified? Again, no hinterland, only successive near 'modernism' in time and taste.

At least as much as the other channels, Channel 4 is addicted to competitive *Guinness Book of Records*-type programmes: the biggest this, the smallest that. ITV's latest is 'Britain's Brainiest Children'. For inhumane tastelessness, Channel 4's latest proposal puts it in the lead: cannibalism on a baby.

An even more recent report, if it is accurate, is even more directly worrying. The channel was negotiating to screen V. S. Naipaul's *A House for Mr Biswas*. It was reported that likely advertisers complained that such a programme, since its characters were all Trinidadians, would not attract a sufficient audience. No doubt its would-be producer was disappointed but the channel agreed to drop the proposal. They presumably agreed with the advertisers or felt it politic to agree. But would at the very least a sizeable audience (if not one of the size the advertisers wanted) have watched? That seems likely; the book had been a great success. Wasn't this the kind of initiative hoped for from the 'free' Channel 4 when it was founded, a well-worthwhile gamble? The clear tie now existing between programmes and advertising revenue even on Channel 4 was there seen in action; practising a kind of censorship, not political but based on low presumed numbers. Who is now the 'conscience' of that channel; who holds the memory of its origins?

'The Public Interest', we have seen, is often a euphemism for sensationalism. Yet it should, as I have already said and will probably say again, imply more than what I already know and like; it should imply what I do not yet know, and might or might not like, but should know for its own sake and ours. So the public service in broadcasting requires from professional broadcasters that they cast their bread on the waters. No less.

Before looking directly at the nature of 'dumbing-down', it would be fair to agree, once again, that British broadcasting in the past and in the present, transmits many admirable programmes, over a very wide spread and all well within the public service remit, and across the terrestrial sound and television channels: news, current affairs, documentaries, drama, sport (probably too much), music, comedy, some situation comedies and much else – though many of the more serious in that list are not now regularly transmitted in prime time. This is true, though to a less balanced degree, of the commercial channels as well as of the BBC. Taken as a whole, broadcasting's portrayal of society and its problems much more approaches balance and objectivity than almost all the press; as it should, given its nature.

Dumbing-down

But when you are chasing someone else's commercial tail the formulaic, the stereotyped and the repetitive are hard to escape. If it works for them, let's try something similar and even more spiced. This attitude also shows itself in another direction, from the commercial arm through to the BBC. Do not push out the boat too often, or extend the boundaries, avoid risks, especially at peak time. Shy away from the fact that some initial failures, which seemed to have overestimated their audiences, went on to gain good audiences; that is, not enormous, but good. Bread on the waters, again.

Do not give way to the common mantra: 'If it works, that is, gets large and even appreciative audiences, then it must be justifiable.' I complained to the BBC's director general that the advance promotion for *Lady Chatterley's Lover* reduced it to a steamy sex story. He replied, personally or with the help of an aide, carefully and politely; but the burden of his letter was that nevertheless it had had a very large and appreciative audience. That's all right then. Any well-hyped, sexual come-on, will fare well.

It is doubtful if anyone is saying that the BBC dumbs-down all the time. Yet dumbing-down is to be found in a sizeable handsfull of programmes and that amount is increasing. Once again, its importance is not to be played down or its relative worthlessness accepted by setting against it the numbers of good and sometimes 'heavy' programmes; there is no trade-off there.

Let us be clear, even at the expense of repetition. One is not saying: we want more good, serious programmes and to hell with the popular. One is arguing that all programmes should aim to be worthwhile, whatever their subject or nature. From this perspective, even five per cent of rubbish is too much and ninety-five per cent of good programmes not enough, and do not excuse the five per cent. Nor, it follows, are such programmes excused by the favourite vindication: 'We have to put out such things if we are going to safeguard the licence fee and so our freedom to make "better" programmes.' That evades the real challenge.

We need another title for another increasing type of programme. Not 'dumbing-down' since that usually implies a programme specifically designed for people of little intelligence and low-level interests. Its partner is a programme apparently on a serious subject but watered down, so that it attracts a wider than usual audience because it makes few demands. Such a one would be a programme, suitably souped-up, on opera or Vivaldi or The Impressionists, presented by a 'personality' with little relevant background. Imitation high culture – filletted, boneless. These are not usually examples of 'getting across without selling-out'.

'Dumbing-down' is in part an instance of compartmentalization by education and class; but that is not a sufficient explanation. We have already seen that some in all groups confess to liking dumbed-down programmes as a sort of relief or cheerful messing around in the mud. Nor is it necessarily only what people such as I do not like or greatly respect. An example: Clarissa Dickson Wright presents a programme about the countryside. Countryside programmes can be very interesting. One typical programme of hers focused on fox-hunting, lamented the possibility of it being banned and supported the usual justifications by the hunting lobby for continuing with hunts. Some of the defences were fair, some odd and shifty. I did not find those arguments convincing nor their presentation palatable. But I would not call that dumbing-down, it did not demean anyone or its subject and had its own frankness and honesty. Nor would I call for a balancing programme putting the case for abolition. That would be niggling; there are plenty of presentations in broadcasting and elsewhere putting the case against fox-hunting.

All too obviously, the main impulse behind dumbing-down is the desire among the competitors to gain, keep and increase audiences. It must always seek the mass or as much of it as it can persuade. A much better picture-in-the-head of possible audiences would start by recognising that we virtually all of us at some times belong to more than one audience, to overlapping audiences of various sizes, sometimes to small minorities, sometimes to minorities so big that they are large enough even to be described as one sort of mass . . . but not truly, because the word 'mass' itself suggests a coagulation not a grouping of self-chosen interested individuals. When we do come together, as in some great public occasions, we are more properly described as a majority, even a large or a huge majority, never a mass.

Programmes which assume a low level of education and a narrow range of understanding in their target-viewers; and perhaps, in some others, a level of taste for certain things well below their levels of education or understanding, may start by tickling both kinds of listener or viewer but end by exploiting chiefly the less well-educated. They are at bottom cruel to such participants and this is so even if the participants have gone in 'with their eyes open'. The more sophisticated viewers of the programme justify it and especially the presenter's brusqueness as 'all part of the game'. True; but it's a low game not worthy of anything calling itself a 'civil society'. Much the same can be said of 'Blind Date', which exploit's participants' ingenuousness or yearning for attention or prurience; or of 'Who Wants to Be a Millionnaire?', which exploits the wish for more and easy money by manipulating easy and difficult, indeed sometimes esoteric, questions so that very few are likely to win really substantial sums. Conversely, for some programmes would-be participants have to telephone the programme makers, at premium rates. That could be a good money-spinner for the companies.

Such programmes set people against each other for, in any worthwhile senses, worthless causes. One remembers the tobacco magnate who advised his children against smoking, and wonders whether the makers of these programmes would like to see their children taking part in 'Big Brother', 'Survivor', 'Dog Bite Dog' or other 'reality' programmes which are really melodramatically distorted confections. Programmes such as those assume a variety of undesirable or unhappy characteristics or aspirations in their participants, and assume also that those are shared with – or enjoy being displayed by – most in the audiences. Such is the prevailing atmosphere that by now a great many, sufficient for the programme maker's needs, would see no difficulty in taking part.

Am I implying too high an aim for broadcasters? Possibly. But, to repeat, a useful maxim says: 'Best try to do good or you'll end by slipping into doing bad.' For a foresight of what dumbing-down could become here if its faults were allowed to develop even further, one need only watch the American 'Jerry Springer' show, now available on satellite television in Britain. For prurient prying into private distresses that is at present the worst; a disgrace to any society which shows it. It reveals the shame behind the claim that a particular programme is 'for our collective amusement' (a mollifying phrase), where it really means 'the highest degree and lowest level of peeping-Tomery'.

It seems easy for some people to decide that most others are stupid, and that all kinds of 'dumbing-down' is what they want and all they can take. There is some truth in that, but not much. To stress a similar point made earlier: productions whether in print or over the air which seek huge audiences cannot afford to give a full picture of those audience's interests; a partial picture pays better. They then justify themselves on the grounds that their partial picture is a complete one, and represents the full range of interests and potentialities of their audiences. That is the lie at the heart of much dumbing-down, wherever it may appear. Given the enormous energy devoted to education over the last century, given the traditional more charitable and humane attitudes still to be found across British society, if that lie were true we would – should – be saddened and soiled.

Towards the end of this chapter we had best return to a less sordid level and look again at what is more widely dispersed: unthinking populism. Back first to another aspect of television news: some presenters' adoption of the role of People's Tribune or Finger-jabbing Sergeant Buzfuz; the automatic harrier of authority. Often missing is firm, persistent, intelligent, well-nourished questioning *of all sides*. The late-2002 strike of firemen produced many examples of this. Much sympathetic attention and easy questioning was given to striking firemen around braziers, less attention to the government position and that in a hectoring, repetitive: 'Are you going to do this or that. Yes or no.' Channel 4 and BBC4 did better than most others.

The main six o'clock news reported on an honours list with first and heavy attention to 'celebrities' well before attention – slight, if any – was given to those of distinction in public life or for good works.

Recently BBC2 obviously felt that decisions on the Booker Prize winner had too much of a whiff of elitism about them. So they added 'The People's Booker', which reeks of soft-centred populism, very anxious to be all-embracing. What did they think a phone-in would add to our understanding? One could not guess the exact winners but could easily guess the nature of the books proposed: bestsellers as published each week, month, year. A waste of time. A self-fulfilling prophecy, which blurs the numbers sold with the quality of the works themselves; an incompatibility.

Even more preposterous because more inflated and over-sold like a new fizzy drink was the programme 'The Top 100 Britons'. It was embarrassing to note the depth of ignorance about almost everything historical or with weight. Pop stars and footballers jostled with Shakespeare, Darwin and Churchill. It was an indictment of the critical and imaginative literacy of many – and that not mainly the fault of their teachers, who are fighting a losing battle against the triviality peddled by television, radio and the popular press.

There is about all this an excessive tenderness, even a kind of fearfulness, which can belittle both a subject and its intended audience. A radio discussion on some aspects of the Muslim faith which might be alien to the British sense of human rights satisfied itself with making distinctions between forced and arranged marriages (one bad, the other acceptable) but seemed unwilling to broach the really difficult issue: enforced female circumcision, which is outlawed by the United Nations but which some ambassadors to UNESCO's Councils defend on the ground that it has been decided by vote in the UN's Halls that all cultures are equal.

An American friend argued that the aim of good television would be to persuade more people to switch off because it had roused worthwhile interests outside television, which could not be satisfied by television. He was probably a lone voice in the vast, noisy, clutching wasteland. More realistic is a nice distinction about television made by an American visiting England. Here, his family found themselves 'viewing programmes' whereas in America the aim of the networks was to make you simply 'watch TV'. The latter seeks a continuous unselective process, the former implies a discriminating one. The British are still, on the whole, viewing programmes. The movement towards our becoming 'watchers of TV' is well underway.

In the Spring of 2002 *The Economist* had a long article, well-nourished as to facts, on the future of television. It ended: 'Television will remain primarily a vehicle for mass entertainment. It will still be manipulative and sentimental, voyeuristic and vulgar [as in 'The Weakest Link']. But it will also challenge, disturb and enlighten . . . There are worse ways to spend a fifth of your working-life.' Having it both ways. Manifestly, well-nourished facts are not enough. The mind needs other nourishment. As, apparently, does the governmental mind since it is not opposed to selling British broadcasting interests to American buyers; an historic, social, intellectual and imaginative treason – and from a Labour government.

The Economist simply accepts that mass entertainment is the main purpose of TV. The wider, public service, idea has fallen away. It will fall further as channels multiply, each with its defined target audience. One could argue that cross-channel switching of programmes would at least secure some of our opportunities to be taken by surprise, to see interesting programmes on subjects we did not know existed. But to urge that in the present climate would be to inspire multiple dismissive cries of 'do gooder'.

We should, on the contrary, recognize that, among much else, broadcasting can be the biggest and best arena for exposing false democracy and welcoming its opposite; in comedy as in current affairs.

After-thought

During the writing of this book, Channel 5 television began to change. The first chairman had been Greg Dyke, who left for the BBC. The first director was Dawn Airey, who had announced that the channel would concentrate on 'football, films and fucking'. She subsequently left.

In the last couple of years Channel 5 has begun an important change of character; not entirely, but enough to make observers remark that it was now in some ways aiming to emulate the initial, more serious, character of BBC2.

Was the change inspired by the dumbing-down of BBC1, BBC2, and ITV? That seems likely. Perhaps it is looking for a new audience – some say about three million is possible and bearable – other than that for the three 'F's.

If so, what a come-down for the Big Ones. One almost wishes Channel 5 well, except that in its semi-metamorphosed form it will still only increase that tightening stratification of audiences which their competitors have pushed along; by chasing audience size rather than quality for audiences.

Chapter 6

Language and Meanings

'At the peril of its soul, it must see that the supply [of news] is not tainted. Neither in what it gives, nor in what it does not give, nor in the mode of presentation must the unclouded face of truth suffer wrong. Comment is free, but facts are sacred.

It is well to be frank; it is even better to be fair.'

(Centenary Leader by C. P. Scott in the
Manchester Guardian, May 1921)

Another marmorial utterance there, to join Tawney and Reith elsewhere in these pages. And yet another, from Carlyle in *Sartor Resartus:* 'Language is called the garment of thought: however, it should rather be, language is the flesh-garment, the body of thought.' Last, one neither marmorial nor bookish-sounding but straight from the idiomatic shoulder, one which could rightly join them, the unfashionable voices, but voices which should be remembered: Ezra Pound: '(When) . . . the application of word to thing goes rotten i.e. becomes slushy and inexact, or excessive or bloated, the whole machinery of social and of individual thought and order goes to pot.' We are well on the way.

In the mass society one of the main channels through which the media of communication work is, perhaps surprisingly, words. That might seem either obvious or paradoxical since information technology experts like to declare that print and so books are soon to become obsolete. The paradox is that words today are both neglected in principle and hugely paid court to in fact. They are daily despoiled but secretly admired; they cannot be left alone by the whole congregation of advertising and P. R. people and their related cohorts. As a result; as a result that is of the uses to which they put language, they end – almost begin – by corrupting it; as Ezra Pound insisted. C. P. Scott's message was that to maintain the distinction between opinion and fact was crucial to honest journalism (and, it follows, to any attempt at fair public communication). Tawney used language as an ethical tool; when he described 'triviality' as 'more damaging to the soul than wickedness' the word had weight which most of us, coming upon it today, would try hard to shake off.

Broadcasters' Bad Language

Since the last chapter was about broadcasting, and because broadcasting is the pre-eminent instrument of communication today, it will be useful to look first and further here at broadcasting's current linguistic and journalistic practice (particularly the BBC's, if only because they used to be thought of as the main upholder of good language). That leads above all to news and current affairs transmissions and their editors and sub-editors, as well as to many of their usual commentators and typical favoured personalities. Outside broadcasting, more scattered but more single-mindedly insistent, are the prowlers in the jungle of misused language. Sports reporters in particular live permanently overheated lives and sound like demented grasshoppers.

Overall, the BBC's practice today is poor, simply and slavishly addicted to assuming that whatever is in everyday speech, is right; that whatever new neologism has crept into common use, barbaric or sloppy or plainly misleading though it may be, can, will and should be used. This manner is now so embedded that it would take a modern Bernard Shaw, if we had one, carrying draconian powers, to reform it.

It is said that formerly the BBC, in recruiting news editors, took care to appoint some with university training, so that copy might be widely informed and linguistically literate. That practice, it is said, has now ended – no doubt on the grounds that it was 'elitist'. Instead, the BBC's journalists are almost entirely recruited from the press, often of course from those who have started in the provincial newspapers or the tabloids and climbed to the national press; and most of whom nowadays will know how to write in the populist manner, with its casual language and built-in errors; which it is no longer fashionable to recognise as faulty. How otherwise can one explain the decline? Most of those newsreaders who have no hand in writing their own copy seem to accept whatever they are given, with virtually no indication that much of it is slack and often ungrammatical in a way which matters, not out of pedantry but because it damages thought and so the argument. Or perhaps some newsreaders do amend the copy they are given so that some errors may not reach the microphone. It would be pleasant to think that at least some of them do have built-in linguistic compasses to support their fine voices.

A minor but careless and irritating habit is that of adding unnecessary prepositions or adverbs, one and sometimes two, to verbs strong enough in themselves. So now we usually hear that something has been 'closed up'. 'Closed down' has been common much longer but, though the 'down' is unnecessary, is more sensible than 'closed up'. 'Lose out' may have come from America but is still unnecessary. 'Free up' seems fairly new to Britain, but is by now very popular; no self-respecting newsreader would care to be without that unnecessary addition. Or those unnecessary additions; one sports commentator produced: 'She will end up losing out.' Double added adverbs are even more common, as in 'face up to' ('facing down to' would introduce a new, excessively miserable element), 'meet up with', 'miss out on'; or as when 'react from [or] against' becomes the unnecessarily heavy 'react away – or back – from'.

As I write, an announcer says that someone has 'repeated again' a particular view. Does she mean that he has 'yet again' repeated that view; i.e. for at least the third time? On current practice I assume she has merely added 'again' so as to intensify, and that she means only 'has once again said' or the equivalent.

Contrarily, and I cannot at the moment think of a reason for the change, one reduction, a dropping of the final adverb, has become common. We used almost always to say: 'sorted out'. Nowadays it is being often replaced by 'sorted', as in 'so that's sorted, then'. For once a sensible change. But will it last? It has something of a fashionable air and so may sooner or later be dropped; well, added to again. Could it also be extended by a reversal of meaning, as in 'sorted in'? That could be as logical and meaningful as its predecessor, but seems not to have emerged yet. Its equally brief but defensible cousin in the current language of sexuality is 'score', as in 'did you score?'

Small stuff so far? Yes, but they have their own minor but important place in clarifying language and thought. Given these relativist times, it was inevitable that some modern books on the use of English would advise that all such habits should be accepted if they are in common use. Even if the common use is plainly against sense? As when some Members of Parliament, whom one had thought should know better, always say 'literally', when 'virtually' is logically what they mean: 'My constituents are literally frightened to death.' The argument, commonly made in universities, for accepting the confusion because it often happens, is 'slushy', in Ezra Pound's word. The nice distinction between 'few' (number) and 'less' (volume, bulk or weight) is another small but important casualty. Languages are beautiful constructions, bearers of both logic and imaginative sense, and deserve better than this.

Whispering against the wind? Probably; but worth trying. So, all broadcasters and the rest of us should declare a moratorium on such frequently used, portentous but unnecessary locutions as: 'on a daily/weekly/hourly/regular basis' instead of the single adverb in each instance. This is the day of the smothered adverbs; many people, especially when they are aiming to be pompously public, shy away from adverbs on their own; but they are useful, indeed essential, neat tools. Or there is the equally big bow-wow: 'at the end of the day' for 'finally', or even 'in the end', or the Aldermanic-implied historical vision: 'In this day and age, we . . .' Those are only two instances, but they are two of the most common and grating. To criticise them will be dismissed as niggling and petty-fogging 'in the light of larger problems' – even the least excusable 'at this moment in time'. Hearing that, it is difficult to resist the suspicion that one is not likely to hear much sense from such a mouth. 'At this moment out of time' would be an interesting variant, if rather disturbing. A small gathering to close this section; on one day recently I heard: 'I'm between a rock and a hard place', 'when push comes to shove', 'after all, it's not rocket-science' and 'it's all gone pear-shaped'.

There are certainly worse habits, muddles and ignorances. Of which one of the crudest is committed by many broadcasters: the misuse of the word 'ethnic'. 'Ethnicity', belonging to each particular race, is common to us all. From the way the word 'ethnic' is applied now, many of its users think it means anyone not of *our* race (or ethnic strain), outsiders, other breeds; and the implication is very often that 'ethnics' (now commonly used as a noun) are slightly lower; though of course that will usually be denied.

A recent television news presenter referred to an aeroplane which was 'carrying many people of ethnic background'. One is bound to wonder to what background it was thought the other passengers belonged – probably British, or Canadian or American (English speakers all); or . . . French? Italian? German? The water becomes very murky here. That those other passengers were assumed to be British, or perhaps groups admissible by the British, is made even more puzzling by another BBC speaker reporting on the audience at a public meeting. They were, he said, 'ethnics, with a few British'. No French, Irish, and so forth, or were they in that instance assumed to be included in the 'ethnics'? Probably not. It was a meeting in London, so one may ignore the odd Dutch, Swedish or Italian persons, if any were at the meeting? But surely, one must assume that other Western Europeans – or all members of the European Union – are not 'ethnic' in the restricted sense used above; so perhaps the word is, after all, a secret synonym for 'non-whites'. If not that, then the use of the word becomes a badge of enormous exclusion, of privileged minority status held by the British. Or perhaps that use of 'ethnic' now begins to show itself as meaning: 'coloured people of all kinds and originally from a long way off'.

Just a couple more examples to reinforce the point that this misuse is common. Another BBC newsreader had a text which reported that 'three of the five came from ethnic backgrounds'; and the presenter of a weekly chat-show similarly said of a certain group that 'forty per cent came from ethnic backgrounds'. Those are merely a selection from a large number of instances. Why have the British become so interested in, so aware of, ethnicity and its differences that they feel moved to mention it so often? And why do they so much assume that it refers to anyone but themselves (exceptions being silently made for some other 'whites'). We are not ethnic, we are in some way free of ethnicity, which tends to be black or brown; we are pure white. It may well be that the immigrations of the last few decades from Africa, the Caribbean and Asia has inspired the recent common use; as a sort of backlash.

Perhaps more importantly: why has the BBC apparently not told its staff at all levels and of all kinds that we are all ethnics together and that, if they want to express our differences from other races, they had better find other words for our condition

145

or theirs? So long as they don't slide back into 'wogs' or 'coons' (which are still unabashedly heard on the football terraces and in too many other places).

Shortly after the battles in Kosovo began someone, I seem to remember it was a Cabinet Minister, introduced the word 'humanitarian'. That was a proper epithet for the action he was justifying. The word proved to be enormously attractive, and was repeatedly adopted. From then it occurred in virtually every report from that theatre, over-used and as often as not ill-used. It is a perfectly good adjective to describe an attitude, a spirit one may try to uphold, or the way in which one describes the activities of some charitable enterprises. Many broadcasters, and soon print journalists, seemed to think it was a catch-all word for almost any aspect, though often a dreadful one, of a war situation. One even spoke of mass murders in a village as a 'humanitarian assault'. It was certainly human though not humane, it assaulted the humane and indeed the humanitarian spirit. It was in itself quite the opposite of a humanitarian act. The word was frequently misused in much the same way during the operations on Afghanistan. Most often it was applied to assaults by those attacking the Taliban. They were 'humanitarian assaults'. This is to twist the word damagingly. They were assaults in the pursuit of victory in battle and neither humanitarian nor humane. They were inevitably bloody and awful. Their hoped-for end might have been 'humanitarian'; but that is another matter. The word has in these instances become part of a horrible oxymoron, at the side of the awful 'friendly fire', for misdirected fire which kills our own troops, and is not at all friendly. That last is an inexcusable invention.

Miscellaneous Linguistic Misbehaviour

Now to the more general exploitation of language; in particular, to 'soundbites' of various kinds; I will use that label rather widely, to include both new sayings which may come to have the status of apophthegms and single, hyphenated or twinned words. Some are wittily concise and may last, though hardly any as long as universal aphorisms such as 'water under the bridge' or the ethically inescapably correct 'two wrongs don't make a right'. That is not the nature of most new formulations. Still, they can be inventive, anonymously: 'he's lost the plot', 'it's not quite rocket-science' (exceptionally popular throughout 2003), 'when America sneezes, we all catch cold', and 'he's doing a wobbly' are likely to have a modestly long life. Others very soon fall off the edge of popular language through massive over-use or because they are too dull to last long. But the general, the fundamental, characteristic must be that even initially acceptable soundbites, though after intensive use, are expendable, among that list of things likely to be quickly worn-out and discarded. Sometimes they go because they were once too much up-to-the-minute, that doomed them; they became 'past their sell-by-date'. They were true products of the mass media society; their's is a brief flight. They enter a kind of linguistic outer-space, forever circling like bits from worn-out small satellites, the rubbish of the verbal universe in which no one has any further use, or interest.

Many of those which last longer seek to describe a new feature of our lives; so 'user-friendly' and 'a window of opportunity' (from the very brief views from circling spaceships) have probably come to stay. Or they wittily or in another way memorably touch, even illuminate briefly, a more permanent element in our lives wherever and whenever we happen to live. 'All smoke and mirrors' is probably derived from conjuring but came into use in the 1980s as a finely compact suggestion of elaborate deceit and looks likely to have a longish, discriminating run. 'Going pear-shaped' is popular and puzzling; it seems to mean that matters are getting out of hand, that everything is sinking to the bottom. I would not predict a long life.

It is intensely difficult to discover those wits who can invent such phrases. It is just as hard to identify those new phrases which are worth keeping and may well last. Who can say? Who or what determines their longer life when so much in this field is devoted to the cycle 'invention > heavy use > end of use'? Do they remain because there are enough 'common users' who instinctively recognise their value? They belong to the oral rather than the printed world, so may have no literary admirers to help retain them.

A phrase which became popular two or three decades ago, especially as forcefully used by Neil Kinnock, the then Labour Party leader, has now faded: 'no more Mr Nice Guy'. That seemed worth a longer life, other than in holes and corners. At almost the other extreme is one still alive and apparently with staying-power, the gruesome 'quality time', which sounds like an advertisement for a patent medicine tonic or for a health-inducing electric exercise gadget. Originally it meant time spent with the children after parents have come home from their offices, but is now more widely used. Its sister is 'Happy Hour', early evening, when pubs and bars try to tempt us in with reduced charges. It belongs to the same over-sweet linguistic underworld as Tony Blair's announcement quoted earlier on the death of Princess Diana, that she had been 'the People's Princess'.

Soundbites usually centre on a single image; many of today's favourites are not older than the start of the last century; some very much younger; say, from about the 1960s, when we began to feel more prosperous. Others obviously due or overdue for retirement include: those chairs on the Titanic, which is outstandingly past its prime and only likely to be used by the lazy; 'let's leave that on the back burner' (very homely); 'piss up in a brewery' and its variants, all very threadbare; 'one sandwich short . . .' Dozens of others, all due for dropping include: 'more than you can shake a stick at [or] than I've had hot dinners'; 'I'm over the moon' (routinely over-used, for anything from a birth to a Lottery win); so are comments on some excess, ending: '. . . as though it was going out of fashion [or] as though there'll be no tomorrow'. And also: 'an accident waiting to happen'; 'that's the worst-case scenario'; 'the Devil is in the detail'; and 'it's as slow as watching paint dry' (from cricket to debates in the Lords to a television situation comedy). 'The jury is still out on that' is a favourite of commentators and columnists; as are 'you couldn't have written the script for that one' and – oh dear – 'it's not over till the fat lady sings'. More recently common in this area are: 'he knows where the bodies are buried', Harold Wilson's 'a week is a long time in politics' and Denis Healey's favourite 'when you're in a hole, stop digging'.

Some are slightly more interesting, inventive or evasive, such as the rounding-off phrase to a shaky argument: 'it's as simple as that' – a sure sign that, whatever 'it' is, is not at all simple. Another which has come into favour fairly recently, at least among politicians and political journalists, and which still seems quite witty is: '[that] is part of the problem, not the solution'; and an MP's current favourite: 'we must draw a line in the sand there'. Odd. It sounds as if determining a firm limit; but lines in the sand are above all shifting, erased twice a day as Canute knew.

Also much heard on television, especially when someone is asserting that they were deceived or otherwise had been done some wrong is 'I've been to Hell and back', which often sounds overblown ('gutted' is its partner) so that one wonders whether a claim for damages is being prepared. 'You're moving the goalposts' sounds as often like a plaintive populist cry as an accusation of sharp practice. Its equally plaintive levelling cousin is 'but it isn't a level playing field'. More attractive and worth a fairly long stay is 'I can't quite get my head round that'.

Local officials, being interviewed in public, tend to reach for the well-educated image which they would be unlikely to use at home or even in the office. A local government official, asked on the radio how he handled two slightly contradictory clauses in a new instruction from Whitehall, answered, 'I was caught between a rock and a hard place there.' There, he joined a club.

Many of the above and dozens of others are, it is easy to see, attractive at first hearing – some are witty and inventive, others cogent, yet others 'right on the nail'. Some have years of useful life before them; others will be thrown away within a decade. Most professions have their own favourites and so do most classes, but all are inclined to 'use them to death'. It really is past time that all of us looked at most of them twice before using them yet again.

One can add here a slightly deviant form; not sentences or whole phrases but single or twinned or hyphenated words which appear from nowhere, cling to everyday speech for a while and then are, most of them, retired. As this is being written, there are of this kind: 'robust' (anything usually described as 'in good health' or 'energetic', or, even more up to the minute, 'aggressive', as in 'I gave them a robust answer'); 'transparent' (longer than 'obvious' or 'clear', slightly technical and more impressive, hence useful when defending company accounts); 'awesome' (almost anything quite impressive, especially the goal in a football match which wins the game – not much left for cathedrals then); and 'step-change', which is used of virtually any change but seems to imply something more, even what others would call, perhaps with more justice, 'exponential change'. Another mixed bag includes: 'bright' (a slightly better-behaved brother of 'smart' which can have slick connotations); 'vibrant' (sounds like a vibrator and from a similar world); 'mainstream' (succeeds 'modern', 'up-to-date'); 'life-style' (life lived according to current taste); and 'attitude' (as a good thing to have in itself; attitude 'to what' does not need to be explained; it is talking about a position, a readiness to accept the world it is inviting candidates to join – in this instance, commercial television – they should apply if they 'have attitude'). At a higher level, there is a favoured word which indicates a sophisticated response to challenging circumstances. Chief executives under pressure tend to use it nowadays to indicate that they are not weakening: 'Oh, I take a *relaxed* (or *comfortable*) approach to that matter.'

'Situations' proliferate, whether or not they are needed; as in 'the classroom situation', 'the learning situation' or 'the marriage situation'. An MP told the world recently that he was 'in a denial situation'.

Political correctness in speech has caused some professions to overreact. I recently had a conversation with a bank official which proved to be full of strange and cautious locutions and individual words, ending with my asking him if the organization he had just mentioned – Saga – was the one which addressed itself to 'elderly' people. 'With respect, Mr. Hoggart, we do not say "elderly". We prefer "mature".' It was tempting to reply, donnishly, somewhat like this: 'But I, for example, am "old"; yet rarely feel "mature".' Corporate language is riddled with face-saving, linguistic woodworm. Estate agents have long been the worst offenders here; and the pompous anonymity who requires us to *aff*-fix stamps on his return envelopes.

The narcissism of mass society, mentioned earlier, is well illustrated in a BUPA advertisement which has just come through the letterbox, a gem of P. R. writing for the present: 'There are times when it's fine to be *self-centred*.' That should assuage any lingering doubts we may have about the ethics of private medicine.

One could fill a whole new section with phrases favoured by those intellectuals who cling to them as an indication of their having read difficult theoretic books: 'polysemic', 'holistic', 'hegemony' and 'paradigm' . . .

Other favourite words are merely silly evasions or seriously deceptive. Silly is the blanket use of 'executive' to make a lowly job seem more important. 'Commercial traveller' long ago gave way to 'sales representative' and that to forms such as 'travelling executive'. By now that last word has become so devalued that few self-respecting *real* executives would want the label, but may accept 'chief executive' which has almost replaced 'managing director' and suggests at least being top of a heap, which runs from 'hygiene supervising executive' (cleaning the loos) all the way upwards. But there is no profit in flogging this live mule.

Much more important is the weaselly evasion contained in the not yet entirely disgraced title of 'developer', or perhaps by now it has in some places become 'senior development executive' or, even more escapist, 'chief environmental planning executive'. Better would be 'chief environmental-rape officer'.

For, in general, developers are exploiters – the only things they seek to develop are their own bank balances. At a time when, though belatedly, we are beginning to recognize the risks to our environment and in particular to the countryside and historic sites and buildings, developers are as severe a danger to those concerns as foxes are to hens. Developers are indeed human foxes, out for all they can get, and giving at best slight lip-service to environmental issues: 'After all, I've got my shareholders to consider.'

A slight but typical instance. We once had a small piece of land at the bottom of the garden. It was important to a would-be developer because, if gained, it would have given access to plots on either side and so allowed him to put four or five Queen Anne executive, four-bedroom, twin-garage, properties – and make a considerable amount of money. The loss to all three of the households concerned would have been considerable since it included access to open land for walking, a consideration which had moved them all when buying those homes. The smoothie pursued us in person and by letter; he suggested a surprisingly large sum for each piece of land. He was relatively young and had not by then learned the language of false sympathy with environmental concerns. He was baffled: how could anyone forgo sums of that size in favour of keeping easy access to a field path and a view for themselves and others? I do not remember seriously using this word before but here it fits – the only arguments he understood were *mercenary*, and in that he may be assumed to be typical of many in his trade, who would be better called simply 'exploiters'. It would be useful if those who seek political correctness in language (who have had some worthwhile victories) turned to such unacceptable words, from those which often reveal unconscious insensitivity, to those which blatantly carry a moral falsehood, as here.

How does one approach the ubiquitous use of the word 'gay' instead of the plain 'homosexual'? From the moment 'gay' began to be regularly used in England I have stuck with the unambiguous word, not out of disapproval but for the sake of the language. An American friend told me he could hardly discuss Yeats's lovely late poem *Lapis Lazuli* with the lines: 'Hamlet and Lear are gay/Gaiety transfiguring all that dread' without giggles from the class. There are other instances; any one example is enough to make a lover of language and literature refuse to adopt the casual extended use of 'gay'.

Some claim it is a cheeky appropriation by verbally clever homosexuals in California two or three decades ago. The trail is longer and more complicated than that. Some dictionaries date its current use from the early 1900s and report that it only became widely used, with its present connotation, after the Second World War. That is slightly earlier than I have known it. There have been other sexual uses, also noted in some dictionaries; as in the early 'a gay house', meaning a brothel. So perhaps the mid-twentieth century use of it was picked up from one of those earlier sexual uses but now applied only or predominantly to homosexuality. In any event, my own objection stands; overwhelmingly the word has in life and in literature and for centuries meant 'happy . . . light-hearted'. In thirteenth-century Old French 'gai' meant just that state of mind. I will continue a modest minority campaign to recover it. And will continue to claim that of all places the BBC's easy adoption of the now fashionable word is another example, but one more distasteful than most, of the corporation's giving in to fashion at the expense of care for the language and the literature.

Is there any point in raising at this stage the misuse of 'hopefully?' Perhaps not, the misuse has spread too far, is too well-rooted by now. A friend who contributes to the work of the Oxford Dictionary told me almost twenty years ago that it was a lost cause. Still . . . 'to travel hopefully is . . . ' uses the adverb in its proper sense, meaning the way we do something, here the manner in which we travel. A starchy old don met one of the common new uses when interviewing a post-graduate student. He asked when the thesis would be ready and had the answer: 'It will hopefully be ready in Spring', to which the don replied: 'Let us hope its hopes are fulfilled'. Encarta suggests that 'let us hope' should be rediscovered and 'hopefully' returned to its original use. Some hope.

The numbers of soundbites listed above and many others reveal double origins. Some have been drawn from old aphorisms and so from older cultures; they are bedded in long experience. Others have been invented by today's persuaders and so are rootless in that they emerge from the demands, the efforts at communication, of this consumer society. They are often meritocratic, or they have a sort of classlessness, but usually imply social stratification. They are virtually homeless and so the more easily cast out when we are tired of them; most have no staying power. Good.

The larger and more important concern about the insults to language is that when it does try to marshal itself so as to meet an issue of great emotional concern it cannot do so; it falls into misattribution and bathos. Since America is at the head of the mass societies and the mass media, and since that country recently suffered one of the most dramatic and horrible of all disasters in peacetime, examples may well have been expected to come from there; and do.

Soon after the announcement of the destruction of the World Trade Centre the Presidential Office denounced 'the cowards' who had committed it. By what twist of language could the per-petrators be called 'cowardly'? Evil, monstrously evil, perhaps; or monumentally misled; but what does the word come to mean if it includes people who for a cause, and perhaps for an assumed paradisal future whatever it may be, are prepared to sacrifice their own lives? This choice of words is like that of a man des-perately rowing for the Shore of Monumental Meanings, who picks up a folded tabloid newspaper to row with.

That was matched by a later announcement which praised 'the enormous heroism of those who died'. Some caught in that awful catastrophe may well have acted heroically; that is likely. Many would not have had the opportunity, being killed instantly. Many, perhaps most, would have been 'frightened to death', panic-stricken, as would most of us. Some, as was seen in the most shocking of all the photographs of the event, even jumped from enormous heights 'for their lives', as we tend to say on similar but much less doomed occasions. On this occasion, that phrase would not have applied; death was certain. To call even such people 'heroes' was another crude misuse of language and not a tribute to them. Against such misuse the ubiquitous bland insincerity of 'have a nice day' and 'enjoy your meal' are insignificant.

Words and Morals

Behind this abuse of language which is typical of mass societies is a condition whose presence has run through these pages. In a time of relativism we have no language for judgement; except those judgements which are echoes of easy and unchallenging popular presentations; which let us down lightly as to a verbal feather-bed; no uncomfortable parts. Since there is no comfort-able place for the noun 'judgement', we deter attempts at it by invoking the handy adverb 'judgemental', which indicates a thoroughly unpleasant and unacceptable attitude.

Any writer who wishes to draw on the concepts of traditional morality has to try to forge his own words or insist that old ones are still currency, defining and redefining them on the run through repeated use in particular senses; old words may be brushed up so as to enter the New World, with weight. Such words as 'decent', which I find myself too often tempted to use both for itself, as a very good word with a distinguished history in both our literature and everyday language, and for its particular connotations from my own experience. It was a pivotal word of choice in my childhood; we trusted it and those to whom it could be applied. We said 'that's not *fair*', or 'that's not *right*' with assurance, invoking an external register. Then there was 'fair-minded', another old and handsome favourite; or 'upright' which has even more something of a Chapel whiff; and, of course, 'honest', and 'honourable'; 'conscience-stricken' (that will take a lot of fitting-in), 'duty-bound' and 'as good as one's word'. Then one remembers the advertiser's motto: 'legal, decent, honest and truthful'; there's misappropriation for you.

Such words if used in earnest are likely to draw dismissive rejoinders of the sort: 'old-fashioned, 'fuddy-duddy', 'stodgy', 'spoil-sport' and the rest. They have to be rejected, or else the dismissers' own kind of chaos will threaten. Current unpleasant phrases from that world are: 'get a life'; and, of course, 'you aren't living in the real world'.

At such times one remembers, for instance, Tawney's magisterial dismissal; not of explicit evil but of something more insidious 'triviality'. That recalls the argument of the preceding chapter, on 'dumbing-down' in broadcasting; and suggests that Tawney's pronouncement should take its place with Reith's and Scott's, also quoted earlier. All of them are or should be powerful, and are well-taken.

Not that that judgement will be accepted by defenders of the present state of things. Too much is at stake in their comfortable view of the world to allow that kind of rethinking. Tawney on triviality was quoted in the 1962 Pilkington Report on broadcasting, some years before we thought of the likely appearance of 'dumbing-down' on the BBC. A celebrated journalist of the day, now dead, invited his readers to mock the report's 'high-minded puritan thinking'. Perhaps even he would have found that stance, and the root and branch dismissal of that word, 'triviality', and others like it, more difficult to adopt today. Or perhaps not; perhaps by now he would have been even more dismissive.

Language is a moral instrument. It is important to avoid its trivial uses and to try to reinstate its organic relations with judgement.

Chapter 7

Gains and Losses

'Change is not made without inconvenience, even from
worse to better.'
(Richard Hooker, cit. Preface to Johnson's *Dictionary*)

'If you know of a better 'ole, go to it.'
(First World War cartoon caption)

Benefits

Anyone who writes critically about the condition of 'our democracy' today is sure to be labelled 'anti-democratic'. In some, that
will be a routine response; in others it will be inspired by their
recognition of the social gains of the last decades; understandably, since there have been many obvious benefits. Why stress,
they feel, your idea of the obverse side of things, and with so little
qualification?

The short answer is that, since so much in modern communications of all kinds is Panglossian, there is ample room for a
record of the other side of life. The longer answer will, in the
interest of balance, be listed below. Each of the gains has also its
qualifying side so, once more in the interest of counter-balancing
and in spite of accusations that an ingrained habit of adverse criticism is still too much on show, those qualifying sides will also be

158

noted. This is a summary of the main elements which are helping to create an open but stratified, a populist though professedly democratic, an increasingly relativist society.

In general, our health is much better than it used to be. Comparisons with the poor condition of many of the conscripts in the last war make that point; it had been even worse during the First World War. The need and the improved response to it can be seen in, for example, the crowded eye clinic of any large hospital today. The National Health Service is hard-pressed and criticised by many, some of whom have political reasons for arguing that it is on the verge of collapse. Overall, it is an admirable model of its kind, and most of those foreign Health Services usually set against it as better examples have disadvantages which are not so often mentioned.

Again in general, we are much better housed than we used to be. The housing legacy of the Industrial Revolution, especially in the Northern cities, was appalling. Go now to a place such as Hunslet, in Leeds, or any similar pre-war working-class district, and try to envisage the mid-nineteenth century, crowded, smoke-blackened terraces of back-to-back houses without bathrooms or indoor W.C.s; and look at the new semi-detached housing where those old houses used to stand. The gain in the houses themselves and in the implied attitudes towards those for whom they were built is evident. So are the labour-saving and 'quality of life' additions: washing machines, refrigerators, microwave ovens, televisions, video-players and the rest in a long line.

Before reaching grammar school I was in a local 'elementary' school with large classes, in an old, cold building, staffed by some who had been inadequately trained and some not well motivated, and some devoted to work in poorer districts. The access to education beyond fourteen hardly existed. For most pupils the future was plain; heavy industry until retirement, then the state old-age pension and a meagre 'going on' until death. For such children access to the grammar school was virtually not a prospect. I was the first to go from Jack Lane Elementary School to grammar school and that was by the headmaster's intervention after I had failed the maths paper in 'the 11-plus exam'. Others reached that 1904 Act grammar school from elementary schools in better 'catchment areas' (mainly lower-middle class or firmly respectable upper-working class), or because their parents, or grandparents, paid the small fees. The comprehensive *idea* is much better; its success harder, than we assumed. Beyond that, there is today much wider access to all types of higher education; plus the outstandingly successful Open University. Whether the assumed orders of merit between universities operate today as stiffly as they did when I started work in the late 1940s I am not sure.

Wages today are for most people much better, absolutely and relatively. Which, as has been said at length earlier, has led to all kinds of new ways, not all of them regrettable, for drawing the money from pockets. But at least people have a sort of choice, one not decided in advance by a restricted and restricting range of what can be afforded, by 'their – "our" – kind of people'.

Of that, the most striking example is the enormous rise in foreign holidays over, in particular, the last forty years. In Hunslet during the 1930s most could not afford even an English holiday unless it was with relatives in another city or even in the country; many of the affordable boarding houses were 'not much to write home about' (some would not let you in during the day unless you were on full board; but usually relented if it rained). To have the sun and warmth assured and at a price you could afford – often for no more than for a week in Blackpool – was a great gain. So more than one Mediterranean coastal village exploded with high-rise buildings.

For women, some qualifications aside, the gains have been greater than those for men, as they needed to be. They start with the introduction of the contraceptive pill and, branching from that and other influences (notably, feminism, as it filtered down), have gone on to produce the substantial increase in part-nership rather than marriage. That is on balance a good change, especially for the woman; if things go wrong there is a way out. Since some men in all classes, but especially the more macho men in the working-class, behave selfishly, partnership rather than marriage can be a salutary condition. To it can be added the great increase in women working and, usually, bringing second wages into the home. It would be interesting to know exactly what are the favoured ways of disposing of that, when the husband is working. If he is not, then obviously the wife's or partner's wage is for fundamental costs rather than for a car [not new] or a foreign holiday, or a brand-new up-to-the-mark kitchen. In addition, women are more and more taking over pro-fessional jobs at virtually all levels; not as much as they should – and will – do, but to an extent hardly conceivable, say, thirty years ago. A few are already at board level, especially those with powerful financial skills as accountants or economists, or as high-level planners or public relations advisers.

These changes in the lives of many women should obviously be welcomed, especially by more men; but some men fail to recog-nize them and continue to act as though nothing has happened. Their wives may be at work and bring in extra money. But some men's assumption is: let them not think they can escape respon-sibility for work in the household when they come home each day. Some women put up with that.

One of the most important changes since the last war, and it has something to do with the increase in comparative affluence, but more to the increasing sense of populist-democracy, is the decrease in the sense of deference. Barbers and a few others still call you 'sir', but that is bound up with the very personal-service character of their jobs. Otherwise, the salutation is likely to be 'mate', and the assumption of a kind of equality. This new mode has a number of sides which some find hard to bear. But even ghetto-blasters on the beach, rip-roaringly souped-up motorbikes and other unattractive elements are more bearable if one regards them as signs that much of the old sense of class-status, of 'knowing your place' and staying within it, has been eroded. In my childhood home, though we clung to our sense of 'self-respect', we always had a mental picture – a sense – of where we were in the hierarchy and what little chance there was of breaking out. That that sense should by now be so much reduced is a main gain over recent years, but to be set against less desirable changes such as, paradoxically, the increase in profit-interested phoney-equality.

Qualifications

So, there are considerable gains. But, inevitably, they have their obverse or darker side. Such as that division in the Health Service. Increasing numbers pay to 'go private'. Interestingly, when a really serious condition arises it is common for such people to move to the National Service. Even intelligent people who may not themselves pay for private medicine will sometimes justify it on the ground that it relieves the strain on the NHS. That argument stands only if you believe that all those who are now servicing private medicine would simply disappear if it did not exist; many perhaps going to richer areas overseas. Not at all; those, probably the majority, who decided not to emigrate or not to try to manage on private work alone, would be available on the NHS; which could then shorten its waiting lists according to need and urgency rather than, as is built into private medicine priorities, by ability to pay. Doctors have and would keep good salaries.

The worst aspect of immediate post-war housing was the creation of tower blocks, those thin giant rectangles usually rising out of derelict areas. That error is by now generally accepted. So is, in the more intelligent parts of the architectural profession, the remarkable blindness to the character of the culture, which was denied, ridden over, by those who designed those blocks.

Some were even highly praised at the time, by the architectural press, and won awards. The majority of those who were put into them soon found little to praise. Many became warrens of 'un-neighbourly' living, dirty and dangerous. In an earlier chapter it was argued that one valuable initial question broadcasters might ask themselves was: 'Do I like the idea of this programme? Does it seem worthwhile to me?' The equivalent question architects might have asked themselves as they designed tower blocks, should have been: 'Would I be happy to live with my wife and family in such a place?' The tower blocks were, apart from all else, embodiments of a divided society, in which one half did not know how (in a more than material sense) the other half lived, and did not try to find out.

Here we come upon a sort of paradox, or unexpected unhappy result. When a conservative government introduced the right to buy your council house many tenants agreed. The terms were favourable, the wish to own and look after your own home was widespread; many of those owner-occupied houses now look better than when they were being maintained by their local authorities. It is not difficult to see why many tenants took out a mortgage and bought. But one step forward, half-a-step back. The result is that council houses to rent are now scarce and waiting lists long. This problem may be partially solved by various kinds of housing trust, and the Labour government is now prom-ising to build many more 'affordable' houses; but it will take a long time to clear the new backlog. The Conservative Party, on the other hand, has promised that housing trusts will be required or persuaded to sell houses which are at present rented. This is political prejudice blind to social concerns; it would further disadvantage those already quite unable to buy.

About education, the problems are for several important reasons larger and even less tractable. Some comprehensives, especially those in more or less middle-class or mixed-class dis-tricts, can work well. They contain parents who are articulate, ready to become involved in the affairs of the schools and used to complaining if any fall below their desired level. Some others in deprived districts work well too, but all there have huge problems, often increased by both the immigration of refugee families, so that a score of languages may be initially spoken by the pupils in one class, and by the emigration of some families who can afford to move to a district with more successful, less stressed, comprehensives. Other parents pay the newly enlarged corps of private tutors, to try to ensure their child wins a place at a selective school not too far off. The English capacity for creating new forms of divisiveness has come into play again. We will have to wait, hopefully but very guardedly, to assess the success of the proposed specialist schools or city academies and their effect on the remaining comprehensives.

The apparent wider access to and the increasing number of universities have helped but, for many, opportunity has remained slight. The standard of literacy is, for a sizeable minority, below that needed for a pass mark at sixteen. The standard needed at eighteen is even more likely to be beyond many. These figures are not necessarily an index of natural ability. But at present the cost of university education can often be a barrier also, even for those eligible for maximum help.

Here we return to a subject broached earlier: public schools. Much the most troubling element in the entire educational scene is the continuation of these schools. They are divisive, not only educationally but also socially, and the second effect may be more damaging than the first. Together, they go a long way towards deciding in advance the choice of professions, styles of leisure, place of living, political assumptions, class of marriage and much else. Whatever the professions to the contrary, they still distort entry to Oxbridge and so to some major professions. Whether anything will be done to remove or improve this out-of-date system in the lifetime of anyone who reads these lines is doubtful. They are deeply embedded. In a newspaper during the week in which these lines are written a woman protested angrily: 'We sent our son to Winchester at the cost of many thousands of pounds a year, and Oxbridge won't even give him a place.' What she expected from Winchester and Oxbridge was a guarantee that entry was assured. What she could not accept was that her son, even though Winchester may well offer splendid teaching and even though at least parts of the Oxbridge admission system are still loaded in favour of Wykehamists and some others, had been judged not qualified for entry to Oxbridge. It would be just if somewhere a comprehensive school pupil was so qualified and gained that Oxbridge place. If that young man with well-to-do parents fell ill he would be likely, of course, to have his operation before a poorer person. Luckily, sometimes, the higher education system can work in a fairer way than the two-tiered Health Service.

I have welcomed throughout the fairly generally diffused greater prosperity. But that suggests rather too much. Better to say that very many people are now not so much strained as their parents were who, in a curious and touching phrase, were 'pushed' for money by the end of each week. Now most of their children have at the end of each week something to spare, something left over. In that sense, choices are wider. In another sense, as is also a recurrent theme here, there are many agencies entirely devoted to directing and narrowing those choices so as to fill their own pockets rather than to give good and varied value. Look only at the quality of some much-hyped 'lounge' furniture, or electronic equipment, or double-glazing, or those ubiquitous fitted kitchens or central heating. Sometimes it seems as though we are a nation beset by sharks, preying in particular on the easily beguiled. But so are many other countries, whether or not developed and whether or not capitalist.

The less attractive side of the most popular of foreign holidays is not so much that they do not fulfil their promise to provide sun and sand; most do. It is, rather, the opportunities they miss. They enclose their clients in cigar-shaped metal tubes, rise from the English damp, and a couple of hours later drop them on or near the chosen sunny beaches. If you wish, and most do, you can there find just the food you most like. The local supermarket is stocked with what the English prefer. A wife with husband and three children summed up on television one of the main pleasures of their Costa Brava holiday: 'A fry-up for a late breakfast on the balcony every day. My Mum could only manage it on Saturdays.' That is understandable and moving. A pity, though, that few wish to try local food; or to climb aboard a local bus (not one to sanitized 'sights', expensively provided by the tour operators), and see something of day-by-day life in the hinterland. A pity, too, that those locals who cater to their needs will have such a constricted view of the English. But to expect such changes at present is asking too much.

Peaks and Plains

Religious belief will linger in corners but have to give up most of its influence. Since for most of us religion was a matter of ethics rather than of dogmatic theology, ethics, will be – are already – under threat too. They may appear to last, to be alive, but do so chiefly in forms invented by the spin-masters (religion = religiosity = sentimentality) and worth nothing in true religious terms. Think of Cliff Richard's pop-tune Christmas hymn and, even more embarrassing, Elton John's dripping *Candle in the Wind* in Westminster Abbey during the funeral service for Princess Diana. That went quickly up the charts, and the promoters of course hailed it as one in the eye for the culture snobs. 'Happy-clappy' revivalism comes in here too.

A less important but more strikingly cock-headed example: the British bids being prepared in the competition for the title of European Capital of Culture (2008). Matthew Arnold is routinely mocked nowadays for defining the respect for culture as 'acquainting ourselves with the best that has been known and said in the world and thus with the history of the human spirit'. There is no ambiguity there; it defines culture as the best we have achieved in intellectual (and 'artistic', is assumed) life. Let us therefore leave aside the usual dismissive slang phrases such as 'highbrow', 'elitist' and 'bourgeois'; and try to see what might be meant by 'best'. We need here to bear in mind once again the distinction between elements which are *representative* of something in their culture (such as fish-and-chips to the pre-war English working-class, and curry to their grandchildren) and things which are *evaluative* of elements in their culture; those which interpret, throw light on, lead to an assessment, especially through one of the expressive arts.

Some ethnic groups might have exceptional powers of visual creativity. That will be part of their culture in the anthropologist's sense; and its role within that culture can be defined but may not normally be qualitatively assessed. If it is so assessed then the anthropologist is moving towards other disciplines, which he is free to do. He may be edging towards the method of the novelist by which, to quote D. H. Lawrence again, he is anxious not 'to put his thumb in the scales', not to be so concerned to point a moral that he distorts the truth of what he is aiming to realize. 'Realization' means trying to create through descriptions of his characters, their interactions and backgrounds, a sense of felt, embodied, life. By this stage the novelist and the anthropologist have parted. One then remembers Henry James' advice: 'Don't *generalise* too much in these sympathies and tendernesses – remember that every life is a special problem . . .'

Today it is commonly asserted that a 'culture' includes not only the whole activity of a society, but that all the expressive activities of a society are by the mere fact of their existence of equal worth. This is the 'good of its kind' belief looked at much earlier. That view can reach not so much sad as wrong-headed levels. The artistic director of a theatre recently wrote of: 'The exhilarating truth that Culture can be anything and can include anything.' To an anthropologist, yes, as we have noted. What we may, for the sake of quick clarity, call the Arnoldian view is different; it invites judgement, distinctions of value, of the 'best'. The director's 'culture' includes empty Kentucky Fried Chicken cartons and booze-ups on Saturday nights. Arnold's has a peak, many peaks, and those include Michael Angelo, Mozart, *Don Quixote*. One of its guiding mottos is: 'We needs must love the highest when we see it.'

So we arrive at the English approaches to bids for the title of 'European City of Culture'. A common early approach (some final bids were greatly improved) was memorably if, for all its slangy assertiveness, confusedly expressed by the framer of Liverpool's bid. He was reported in the *Guardian* as saying: 'It's not just the local Crown Jewels. We have to go with a concept of culture that means something to everyone in Liverpool.' That encapsulates perfectly the populist definition, which seems to be shared by many of the dozen applicants. At that stage about half seem to be proposing to offer, as one of their cultural jewels, a pop musician who happened to have been born in the town. About the same number include writers of very different worth who, again, were born in the particular town but almost all of whom soon left it and had their strongest affiliations elsewhere. (C. S. Lewis for Belfast. Oxford, more convincingly, also claim him.) Norwich claims the novelist Kazuo Ishiguro who graduated from the University of Kent and then attended the University of East Anglia's course in Creative Writing; hardly a native. Bradford still claims J. B. Priestley who after the First World War went to Cambridge and then settled in London; and David Hockney who has long lived in California. This begins to seem like misrepresentation under the Trades Description Act. Bristol claims Cary Grant. Astonishingly, Oxford claims only three authors, two from the twentieth century and both dead (C. S. Lewis and J. R. R. Tolkien), plus Phillip Pullman, the author of books for children who in 2002 won the Whitbread Prize; plus a couple of pop music groups and the redolent, catch-all offering, 'dreaming spires'. That is probably the most ridiculous of all the preliminary lists seen.

Matthew Arnold must be weeping somewhere. Whoever drew it up for Oxford seems to have little sense of history, of intellectual and artistic life, of what can on any sensible definition be called Oxford's contributions to British and European and world culture over many centuries. 'Let it all hang out' populism at its worst. One can easily imagine the city fathers of Leipzig, Strasbourg, Florence or Barcelona, as they looked at those lists, rubbing their eyes and then bursting into laughter.

All this in the name of democracy, but not democracy in any worthwhile sense; an ignorant democracy rather, which reduces the best achievements of its own past and at the same time belittles its citizens. Almost all of these lists run against Colonel Thomas Rainborowe's magnificent assertion at the Putney debates in October, 1647: 'The poorest he that is in England hath a life to live as the greatest he.' We must believe that he meant a good not a silly life.

There are more sophisticated examples than those draft entries for the European City of Culture. It is entirely in the nature of the time that Saul Bellow, exasperated by total relativism in a variety of cultural judgements, asked that he be shown the Tolstoy of the Zulus, or the Proust of the Papuans; he would be glad to read them. It was also predictable that Bellow would then be attacked for elitism, for running down Zulu and Papuan culture; attacked by people who seem unwilling to recognize high achievement in literary culture whilst at the same time recognizing other values in largely oral cultures. Both have to be placed on the same level platform. So far as I know, there is no evidence that Saul Bellow does not value Zulu or Papuan cultures. He is challenging, as mistaken, an attitude which insists on valuing all in exactly the same way; it is possible to value an oral culture whilst also recognizing the greater overall achievement, more complex and searching (as in *War and Peace*), of the European tradition. As many an eminent African novelist, who probably draws on the European tradition, would agree.

What about democracy; will that weaken even more? Even as we insistently claim that it survives and is healthy? It will not appear to fade away as secure religious belief is doing. As in fake religions, various simulacra will be offered and each hailed as the one and only true form of democracy. But it will be both a diluted and a corrupted form. It will be, yet again, levelling and populist, without the honest, gritty character of genuine democracy. It will not offer its citizens real freedom of choice – even to go to hell in their own way or, much more day-by-day, to consistently blow the gaff on the powers that be – both of which must inhere in a democracy. Instead, its Gods will be: money, celebrity, power; and all of us equal before the 'hegemony' of the balance-sheets.

It will offer day after day what the persuaders have decided is good for their audiences in the pursuit of profit or of a docile citizenship (the two are naturally intimately related). It will offer at any given moment just what will be absorbed but not cause revulsion: soft porn today, but no doubt hard-core porn tomorrow, violent sex-and-violence dramas on television today but perhaps public executions tomorrow. As we have seen, a key contrast in broadcasting's public service principles is that one should give audiences not only those things they already know they want (inevitably but not fundamentally revised as the years pass) but also offer some good things the programme-makers believe they ought to have but have remained unaware of. With what justification on the part of the programme-makers? Because it is right to offer things of value, things which those who pursue all the time large audiences with items which meet only existing tastes will not offer; but which are instructive, enlightening, witty – whatever particular form they may take, from documentary to comedy.

The decline of religious belief and the rise of a catch-as-catch-can type of democracy, then, together breed relativism in place of firm values. It will be remembered that a special adviser (not a civil servant) in the Department of Transport issued an e-mail on 11 September 2001, the day of the destruction of the World Trade Centre, in which she suggested to her selected recipients that this would be a good day to bury bad news (apparently concerning local councils). The act seemed almost unbelievable. Simply recall the situation on the day. It was announced, in the early afternoon in Britain, that two passenger aircraft had been deliberately flown into the twin towers of the World Centre in New York. The horror was there before us, hour after hour, on our television screens. It was plain from the start that thousands would have lost their lives. Millions across the world felt overwhelmed with near disbelief and horror; an inability to comprehend the enormous frightfulness, a sort of unimaginable, inconceivable, unassessable shock to the mind, at first and for long afterwards. How could anyone at that time feel it right to issue a message advising her recipients that this would be a 'good' day to announce bad news about a local if rather troubling eventuality? Naturally, many people demanded that the woman be sacked by her Secretary of State. She was not, whether because he thought the error did not justify dismissal, or out of mistaken loyalty to one whom he had appointed. It was finally arranged that she should make a public apology to camera; not a reassuring sight. She stayed, though some months later more disputes within the department led to her departure and that of a civil servant.

So much is common knowledge. What I did not read or hear – though I may have missed the suggestion elsewhere – is this: surely in less relativist times such a person would have felt it right on her own initiative, not as a result of polite persuasion, to resign. Shouldn't she, now realizing what the majority of thoughtful people felt about an act which she had apparently assumed to be acceptable, have decided that the only respectable step was then, on several grounds, to resign; for both her own good name and that of the department.

In the background one could hear the usual placatory expressions: 'oh, they all do it, so . . .', and 'That's the way the world is, the "real world".' Not everyone's 'real world', that, but the self-defining and self-justifying world of many people today. At its lower level, it is the world of 'stuff you, Jack, I'm all right', and 'it's every man for himself'; and that one which sounds innocent and easy but is often used to brush aside complexities, especially ethical complexities: 'it's as simple as that'. One can almost hear the doors of the mind closing.

Dostoevsky's Warning

We noted earlier that recent research has shown that many young people aged between seventeen and twenty-four actually believe that their favourite footballers eat *that* cereal and use *that* hair-gel. That is one among many forms of being misled today, but still surprising; and depressing, especially to school-teachers. It is at this point, and the more we look at it the more relevant it seems, that we recall Dostoevsky's warning from one and a half centuries ago: that, in the name of the promoters' freedom to offer and our freedom to choose, we will be lulled with soporifics and so loose our real, our substantial, freedoms: 'Yes, we shall set them to work, but in their leisure hours we shall make their life a child's game . . . Oh, we shall allow them even sin, they are weak and helpless, and they will love us like children because we allow them to sin. We shall tell them that every sin will be expiated, if it is done with our permission, that we allow them to sin because we love them . . . and they will have no secrets from us . . . The most powerful secrets of their conscience, all they will bring to us, and we shall have an answer for all. And they will be glad to believe our answer, for it will save them from the great anxiety and terrible agony they endure at present in making a free decision for themselves.' Strong stuff, but awe-fully prescient. That soporific effect is more likely than the apocalyptic; unless we collectively destroy ourselves.

The process continues and spreads. We have noted recent moves to 'lighten' television news so that people who do not want any 'heavy' news can exercise, assured, their 'freedom' to watch only what pleases them. Soap operas which used to have some weighty elements (carefully mixed with the lighter), have begun to lose those more serious elements in favour of the melodramatic (which is seriousness inflated into caricature). The weightless commentators more and more rule; such as the one who observed on air that the audiences for the film of the sinking of the *Titanic* were relentlessly going up – whilst the ship itself went relentlessly down. You need to have a tasteless mind simply to think that funny, and one even more tasteless to think it worth broadcasting.

Faced with such opinions as those above, some readers are sure to respond 'but you expect too much of ordinary people.' This may be true, but unexpectancy easily slides into expecting too little of 'ordinary people', into easily consigning 'ordinary people' to Dostoevsky's social and moral dustbin.

In a large hospital ward I was the only patient who bought a broadsheet newspaper. The place being a mixed-class part of Surrey, there was a spread of tabloids. I saw only one doctor with a newspaper – the *Daily Express*. I do not assume that the height of social progress will have arrived when we all read the 'broadsheets'. It is plain that they too are affected by current processes. Yet one could fairly feel disappointed by that pattern.

In some newspapers that has been going on for a very long time, long before broadcasting, since at least the turn into the last century. Yet even in the 1930s we had the *Daily Herald* and the *Daily Mirror,* both better than today's popular press. One died, the other changed itself under the pressures of money-driven not quality-driven forces.

One cannot help wishing for a little 'opening up' rather than 'closing down'; and remembering T. S. Eliot on the effects of expecting too little; that it begins by underestimating people and ends by debauching them. That is a form of the truism that if one does not aim a little higher one will inevitably slide lower. If we are not tempted to think outside the boundaries so much set up today, we will settle for the known and unchallenging. So, in the world of the mass media, opinion is subverted into opinionation, sentiment into sentimentality.

This whole process wastes by misuse such education as most people are given; it betrays the clear gifts of some and the potentialities of many; it widely abuses promising resources. Is this really the inevitable, the inescapable, cost of a society which wishes to be correctly called a democracy but cannot find a way both to educate its members adequately and to rein in the worst excesses of capitalism; and some of its media expressions?

Among which excesses is the hidden, complicit censorship noted earlier. I use those two adjectives so as to try to capture the usual nature of censorship today. 'Hidden' because not made explicit; 'complicit' because generally accepted by tacit agreement. One professor of Philosophy temperately criticised and tried to explain the enormous outpouring of emotion when Princess Diana was killed. He was widely reviled; he should not have said those things; he had 'no right' to say such things; the implication from many people, that his words could fairly have been refused by the newspapers, was plain. The death of the Queen Mother in early 2002 produced pages of almost unsullied praise in virtually every newspaper (the *Guardian* had one dissenting article after two days). In general, free speech was blanketed by adulatory mush; anyone speaking against it in public could have been given a hard time. That type of censorship takes the form of group bullying; almost anything which questions the prevailing consensus is roughly blanketed; which is almost always successful.

Desensitizing?

We come now to the hardest question of all and one which it is impossible to answer objectively, actually to weigh and measure. What is likely to be the long-term, though at present partially hidden, effect of today's increasing relativism, this constant drip of loose, unordered but often emotionally violent persuasions on us internally, on our subsequent or eventual attitudes and acts? Are we all affected equally? Probably not. But all to some extent affected? Probably, yes. Even wider: is someone like myself, mulling over so much and so many of the changes described in the foregoing pages, inevitably going to sound like Dickens' Fat Boy; to become over affected, whilst the evidence – so much like a monstrous mound of verbal rubbish – piles up. He sits over the word-processor, largely cut off from most of what must surely be the stabilizing influences of the everyday; in short, is such a writer someone whose arguments can be easily put aside? On that, something in the next and final chapter.

Yet are there some likely effects which can be defined or at least described? Perhaps if things go on as they are, someone will eventually do that. I have to make do with suggesting that, overall, the barrage to which we are all subject – unless we take determined avoiding action, individually and collectively – is likely to have a mesmerizing, a sedating and perhaps in the end what I am provisionally calling a *desensitizing* effect; a numbness in the face of all the violence, the sexual prurience and Peeping Tomery, the titillating of feeling by febrile emotions. Perhaps the increasing lack of interest in the process of democracy itself, the cynical feeling that it's all a con and voting a waste of time, is one of the early signs of this disassociation.

A report from the nineteenth century, about the political and democratic energy of many working people, makes a useful contrast. Henry Hetherington noted: 'In those days of intense political excitement [the early 1830s] the working-classes hungered for political news, and this was the kind of intelligence the paper [*The Poor Man's Guardian*] chiefly gave. It boldly announced in each number that it was "established contrary to law and published despite the laws or the will and pleasure of any tyrant".'

Times have changed, certainly, and partly because of the activities of just such rebels. The shortcomings of our own society are much less evident; but not to be taken for granted or left uncriticized. We must remember our common humanity, our resources of charity, our admiration when we meet honesty and goodness in action – all those things which show up the hyped language and acts of the shallow, the vicious and the violent which are so much fed us today (whether through print or over the air) – and all in the name of 'public interest', confused with 'what the people want'.

The case for gradual desensitization seems nowadays particularly strong: never has so much violence, so cleverly presented, been shown as entertainment on so many millions of screens. Much of it is in a strict meaning of the word 'gratuitous'; made for its own sake or used as an audience-grabber, and presenting a world in which this sort of thing is assumed to be self-sufficient, as entertainment, not something to be assessed within a pattern of pressures, a network of ethical choices, a context in which all choices have their consequences and costs. The debate here as so often is ill, or not at all, engaged. When it does engage, it is usually hamstrung by prior relativist assumptions. If it should be decided to begin the debate properly, perhaps the hidden starting question might be, not: 'how can this possibly have any effect?'; but rather: 'given its frequency and force how could it be without at least some influence?' Loaded? Perhaps, but no more than is that first, usual, approach of today; and demanding just as much effort at objectivity.

Chapter 8

Baggage for the Road

'Reflecting upon the magnitude of the general evil, I
should be oppressed with a dishonourable melancholy,
had I not a deep impression of certain inherent and inde-
structible qualities of the human mind.'

(Wordsworth, preface to *Lyrical Ballads*)

Raw Nature?

An expert in the pathology of habitual and violent criminals,
speaking about one such case, gave me a long-overdue shock;
overdue because I felt I should have known of it or, if it is still in
question, heard long ago of the state of the dispute. He observed
quite matter-of-factly that it was entirely beside the point to argue
with some such criminals about anything relating to their 'moral
duty'; no good for judges to call them 'depraved' or invoke other
condemnations in the litany, or to exhort them to recognize their
'moral failings'. That element in their brains is missing, was so
before birth. So that, however much they may occasionally seem
to behave ethically, that is a form of defensive or deceptive acting
learned from experience, not fed by an impulse in their natural
character; a quality which cannot be induced, and is likely to
express itself as opportunity offers.

I cannot say how widely this view is accepted by pathologists. In his book, *The Blank Slate*, Professor Steven Pinker says that 'it seems' as though psychopaths cannot be cured. If 'nature' were finally proved to be the cause, that would be a chilling thought: briefly, that some people are morally unconscious – better, perhaps, unendowed – and that their condition cannot be radically altered. Perhaps some experts would still deny this and argue that, though such a condition may exist, it can be altered by neurological intervention through surgery or chemistry.

Or we may continue to hope that attitudes which seem amoral may not be inherent, but the products of upbringing and background; and may be changed through education and other non-invasive forms of persuasion. Racism, for example.

If we are finally led to think that the first pathologist, he who studies 'the criminal mind', is right, then sayings I have long liked and taken as guides to aspiration are wholly mistaken if addressed to such people; that sayings such as 'we must love one another', or the schoolroom injunctions to 'aim high' (which speakers at school speech-days are fond of offering), are wholly meaningless to some – if perhaps a very few – people. They may hear them, they may even note that they do affect some others but are themselves unable (not 'unwilling', because that would imply that their brains allowed them to 'will' that way), to interpret such injunctions and act on them, to 'learn from experience'. And, if they do not so act, that they do not feel 'guilty'. Rather, they are of those who have never known 'any world where promises were kept, or one could weep because another wept'.

In childhood and early adolescence I had a simple, a simplistic, assumption: that 'philosophy' was above all about ethics, an enquiry into the nature of 'goodness' and 'wickedness'; and even held at the back of my mind the idea that philosophers were likely to be 'good' people, or people who strove towards the understanding and practise of 'goodness' in themselves. The loss of that idea was initially prompted not by books but by meeting an Oxford philosopher who was, it seemed evident, selfish and cruel; though 'brilliant'.

He has been offset in my mind by two people, one a soldier met during the war, the other a literary scholar. If there is such a quality as 'innate goodness' they had it. They seemed to think little about their own needs and wishes, but to be entirely un-self-regarding. They were not weak-willed or indecisive, but all their decisions were, it seemed, taken for the common good or the good of another. Where two 'goods' might apparently conflict, their actions could often make them seem compatible. Even now, one is tempted to say they were 'good Christians'.

For the purpose of the argument, and because I wish it, I assume that first pathologist to be mistaken in his view that a lack of moral feeling is in the nature of some people and not, at least at present, correctable. I go on believing – well, hoping – that in all of us there is 'a moral sense', whether developed or not, that we have to keep trying to develop it in ourselves and, so far as we can, recognizing and valuing it in others. Where does that poten-tial capacity learn to develop?

Presumably in the family and in society; in both places, for good or ill, and more indirectly than by injunctions. My own 'ethical sense', such as it is and whether I sufficiently heed it or not, may owe much, perhaps its most important elements, to inherited genes; as to that, I can only guess. Insofar as it may be developed culturally, that sense may owe much to our mother who died when I was eight (but her loving and as necessary cor-rective spirit is still alive in me); to my grandmother who brought me up and embodied the upright ethics of Primitive Methodism, to a lesser degree to the substantial morality, which was followed by many, of a 1920s and 1930s Northern working-class district, and to my wife who seems largely to have learned it from her honest churchgoing parents. And, though there were people in working-class Hunslet who had fallen through the sustaining nets which even such a poor district could offer, most there shared and largely obeyed a culture which, from the viewpoint of the early twenty-first century, seems remarkably coherent and – yes – 'moral' in its hidden but not ineffective guides to one's behaviour towards oneself and others. They 'took it for granted' that one tried to follow 'the truth'; which was 'out there', unquestionable. And most who 'fell short' knew they had done so, that that phrase indicated a lapse from a certain truth, a known scale of values; not something uttered as a self-conscious statement whenever occasion offered; but something known 'underneath', and so far as possible to be followed. Yet one or two did seem impervious to ethical injunctions; we usually put that down to their 'upbringing' (nurture), though occasionally one heard of someone who was 'rotten to the core' (which seems to derive from that other phrase: 'a rotten apple'), by 'nature'; and may imply that reform is not possible.

Those first few pages of this chapter took us, I now see, up a side-track. They were about people, a few, who seem to have been born without a conscience, as some scientists believe and others do not.

Obviously, that is a most important question. Yet, again obviously, more preoccupying for most of us is the fact that we do have consciences, but that almost all of us betray them from time to time. The awareness of this runs through our lives and literature, from St Paul through Ovid to Goethe and many another. 'I recognize the good, but do the bad.' That recognition separates us from the apparently conscienceless people mentioned above.

In Christian terms, we are all in a state of 'original sin'. Wordsworth thought his 'melancholy' dishonourable because it ignored better human qualities. Cardinal Newman would not accept such comfort. His appalling statement brings one up with a shudder: '*If* there be a God, *since* there is a God, the human race is implicated in some terrible aboriginal calamity. It is out of joint with the purposes of its creator.' We remember then Ivan Karamazov giving back to God his entrance ticket to life, because he could not accept a God who will allow children to suffer horribly.

Now a more down-to-earth warning to ourselves, as we leave this section. We have to try to distinguish between 'values' and 'taste' or 'opinions', not to seek to turn almost every issue into a moral one. We may like some smells and dislike others, but that is not a moral matter. It might become related to one if a malicious person threw a stink-bomb into our sitting-room. Laziness of speech may have a moral dimension, as Ezra Pound asserted. Regional speech should not be judged, as it often is, on that plane, rather than being seen as a social phenomenon, and criticism of it as an instance of snob attitudes.

Rudderless

It has been argued throughout this book that, with the decline in the prosperous, consumer societies of religious belief – indeed, the decline of the very idea of belief in itself – we are seeing, in some respects have already seen, the beginning of, the early emergence of, relativism as a substitute for belief. This implies the rejection of the idea that religious belief carries with it an accepted scale of ethical values outside ourselves. Relativism implies that circumstances alter all cases. Taken only so far, that last view might be a guide to the need for charity in assessing others; beyond that point it becomes a valueless repudiation of the need for any defining judgement. Since there is no common ground here, can one ever reach the point in which one may ask or be asked (in Dr Leavis's formulation): 'This is so, is it not?' and expect a 'yes' or 'no' answer from within the common ground? In such circumstances some, feeling a need, take up an ideology; which is by its nature firm and close-ended but does not reach out beyond itself, its own earth-bound reasoning and justi-fication.

It is plain that I cannot agree with George Steiner: 'Where God's presence is no longer a tenable proposition and where his absence is no longer a felt, indeed overwhelming weight, certain dimensions of thought and creativity are no longer available' – but I feel the 'weight' of what he is saying. We are here talking about trends rather than about a fully achieved process of change. Individual lives and societies do not change so dramatically quickly. Very many people today seem unchanged, not at all relativist in most of their attitudes. Yet many of us are by now living on our accrued ethical capital, and under pressure that already shows in some of us; both the fact of that pressure and the reaction to it. As usual, favourite expressions, some of which quoted earlier, indicate the way the wind is blowing, as in these and many others: 'they all do it'; 'if I didn't do it, someone else would'; 'that's the way the world wags'; or, yet again, 'that's the real world, isn't it'. And, from a different angle: 'It ain't what you do. It's the way that you do it.' Style before substance. Manner before matter.

There have been many other examples in earlier pages of this emerging attitude. They boil down to a rejection of differences in quality anywhere or in any things, from behaviour (odd populist exceptions of long standing being allowed here, as matters of fact) through to intellectual life and the arts. We are teasing, of course, at the matter of values; of guide-posts which can never be taken for granted; and never be pushed aside. If we try to do that, false values – even the shifty value that is relativism – will rush in and fill the space. The search then for what seem right values has to be a more aware, a critical process, a first cutting away of all the entangling undergrowth of misleading voices and deceptive sign-posts.

This may not mean that most of us will be ethically rudderless. Church and chapel backgrounds do not fade so easily; we will still feel moral compunctions. Insofar as we articulate them, we and our successors will have to make our ethics out of whole cloth. In that, it is clear that we will not be helped by most of the public voices around us. For that, we will need to go to more worthwhile influences and encouragements; from those who will find it much more difficult to secure a hearing from us than do the other, the prevailing, voices. We have to find for ourselves those better, more disinterested speakers. We will need first to look back and try to take hold of 'the roots that clutch', and also to recognize what is or could be made worthwhile in the new world.

Even by now it will be a hard and slow process. Relativism has already put some strong roots down in some places, as is plain every day. Questioned about the rightness of his political party in accepting substantial funds from a man who had gained his money from what could in the old language certainly be called morally dubious means, a Secretary of State replied that it was a mistake, 'stuffy', to bring moral issues into such a question. He spoke with what could be called 'conviction'. He was a product of his day. The memory of Lord Goodman, saying he would take money from the Devil himself if it passed to an undeniable public good, reappears. Even that is a dubious argument, but has some slight justification. The Secretary of State had no such support; he was speaking for the right of competing political parties to get their funds – their 'fighting funds' – from anywhere, without ethical strings.

A few days later, a junior minister was taking part in a broadcast discussion on the ethics of selling arms abroad. It was for most of its time a sober and well-fed discussion. The junior minister had her say towards the end. With the assured forcefulness which many politicians soon learn, she insisted that not to sell arms abroad would be mistaken since it would make thousands unemployed. Of course; and that would be very sad. But it is not properly a contribution to the ethical argument: it evades that. She might have said that all possible steps should be taken

183

to find employment for those made jobless; that would have been an ethical suggestion. But she was stuck up a dead-end.

Only a few days after the above remarkable announcement, at the period of the World Cup football matches, there was, also on Radio 4, a discussion about ethics in football, inspired by what to some spectators had seemed cheating. Of the two speakers, one refused to see that any ethical questions arose. This was a game, a competitive game; you cheated if you could. You had always to remember that if you failed, you would be handed a yellow or a red card, so you played cunningly. The card has become a substitute for a high court judge; or God. The one principle is to avoid being found out. That is all; no rules outside those of expediency; any talk outside that is irrelevant. If that was how that man conducted his daily life in all things; one wouldn't buy a second-hand car or anything else from him. His manner was not defensive and did not give the impression that his views were other than common to all those around him. This was his and others' 'real' and right world.

At what date did it become possible to say that sort of thing publicly, without qualms? Cheating certainly went on in football in the 1930s; it is less certain that someone invited to discuss the issue on air would have done so without feeling that any justification for cheating had to be very carefully made since it raised serious questions not only about football but more widely.

The response of the other speaker underlined how far we have come. He expressed unease but was unable to find words to express it. He had no access to a language of judgement. Nor, apparently, had the BBC's presenter who was guiding that discussion.

In a more confident time, Emerson declared: 'Men are convertible. They need awakening.' Even a professional preacher would hesitate to use such language today. And at most educational levels, there is an almost complete refusal to attend to those questions; understandably, because they are intensely difficult to cope with and would be even if the climate were more open to them. 'Civics' are now rightly being promoted in schools, but should be rooted within, follow from, larger, initial questions; and most teachers would feel ill-equipped to present those.

Parents and Neighbours

If we are parents, the case is different. We do not have constantly to offer our children, for example, a list of commandments; we will inescapably make them aware of values, good and bad, through our own behaviour; and should try to justify them if challenged.

One needs to have in mind from the start that silence – the silence of ill-temper or that of the sense of deep mutual affection – may be as influential as many words. Yet our efforts sometimes, perhaps for most of the time, can seem to have little effect. A friend, the loving father of four children, suggested that the influences on children, whether from nature or nurture, were so numerous and complex that the degree of influence one or both parents might have on each is roughly equivalent to putting a brace on their front teeth. Which recalls Philip Larkin's tender, almost wistful lines about family life, bringing up children, caring for the old, often seeming a little comical, engaged in 'a sort of clowning', but all in all on activities which are worthwhile, meaningful: 'a sort of clowning' can also be a sort of oblique teaching and loving.

Once again, we are in a place where to do nothing does not mean that nothing happens. Children will notice, but may then choose all their guidelines from their peers; and those are usually immature, sometimes deeply misleading and sometimes admirable. We may wish to shrug off all our responsibilities but they cannot be escaped; we are implicitly as well as explicitly, all the time 'giving an example'. We all fall down sometimes, speak and act meanly. To some degree our children may learn that from us, or take the lesson that it is not a good way of behaving. We have all seen parents who seem to have 'given a good example' to their children; and seen from some such homes a child emerge who is, against all apparent odds, delinquent. Yet, and it seems obvious to say so, children from steady, affectionate homes do appear more likely to emerge as, themselves, steady and affectionate. That is a cheering thought.

To take an activity which might seem, before the complexity of the issue, slight, but which is at bottom not at all slight: it is important that parents read to their children, read regularly, and as soon as possible move from books specially written for children to just good books which can be enjoyed by readers of all ages. It almost goes without saying that Dickens is a superb example of this kind of author. Such books must be found enjoyable by the children, must not be overtly instructive, nor be approached like medicine. They have to be read for their own sakes. Much will come through insensibly about the varieties of character and relationships, about place and landscape, the sense of history and time, the regular prat-falls, the comedies, of life; and the weight of the choices with which we are all presented. Again, none of this need be explicit, nor need be actually said, though at its best it will be felt in the mind and imagination. The act of reading and listening helps to bind the participants in a sense of shared pleasure; or perhaps that is too overt a way of putting the experience. It is, rather, a shared experience, a feeling of communion between the child and the adult which arises from the reading, has taken off from the book, but is not necessarily tied to the story the book might tell. The occasion has its own stillness. It can emerge from the act of reading a serious but not solemn book or from a comical but not silly book. It transcends anything called up by the simple label 'reading to the children' but has resulted from that. It is all the more important at a time when so many other experiences, most of them evanescent, are offered to children as much as to adults. It works against much in society which is instantly attractive but of little worth; such as many of the most popular television programmes, whether for children or adults. That, reading to children at home, is one good habit we should hold on to and expand. It is, of course and not surprisingly, a habit which on the whole starts within the lower-middle class but is also followed somewhat higher up.

There are other good, and bad, habits among all classes which seem so far to have resisted more unsubstantial tendencies, or to have adapted new offerings to old practices. We have noted more than once that the British are slow to change, and that this has been a buttress for them. 'Good' working-class and lower-middle class husbands have always been assiduous in 'doing things about the house and garden'. There seems to be little weakening of those practices, especially when council houses have, latterly, been bought by their tenants. The new D.I.Y. superstores have latched on to and developed these long-standing interests. Allotments, where the local councils have been able to hold off the developers, are usually in steady demand. The range of surviving – and new – hobbies is large: cultivating your back garden, breeding prize-winning canaries (that taxi-driver), collecting classical music, not in easy-to-listen-to anthologies (the railway booking-office clerk and a butcher), taking Open University courses . . . one could continue that list for a long time.

Perhaps the most striking survival of all is the sense of neighbourliness, which is different from the 'you-you-you groupiness' to which we are called today. Related to neighbourliness, and most common from the lower-middles to the upper-middles, is membership of a host of voluntary bodies largely devoted to making life more bearable for the deprived, the old, the ill; and to meeting any other need which someone somewhere can spot and decide to 'do something about'.

Here also one should acknowledge – difficult though it can be to avoid sounding folksy and even chauvinistic – the general friendliness and helpfulness which can be met in the streets and shops, the sense of fellow-feeling rather than of suspicion before strangers. Up North it is still enshrined in the word 'luv'. One Sunday I took a train to a hospital in the hills a score of miles North-West of Leeds to see my sister who was very ill. The hospital proved to be more than a mile from the tiny station; being lame, I had arranged for a taxi to meet me there. When the train arrived there was no taxi, and no telephone booth; and the rain was pouring down. A small car drew up and took on board the only other passenger from the train, a middle-aged woman. The driver paused, looked at me and asked where I was going: 'Oh, we can go round that way and drop you, luv. It's not far off our road. We can't have you standing in the rain.' The back-seat was loaded with stuff; which she pushed aside to make room for me.

I know that unsolicited kindness could be found below the line at which they call you 'luv'; it shouldn't be taken for granted anywhere or at any time. All such habits and many others testify to an unarticulated but powerful disinclination to let go of some admirable traditional practices towards others, to that sense of fellowship. 'Going on going on' is not simply a near-instinctive impulse, a disinclination to be kicked off your well-used perch by new-fangled offerings. It is part of a web of valued attitudes which has given support, is still supporting, positive residual strengths, and seems likely to go on providing a bulwark against the oxymoron of solipsist-togetherness which we are all, as a single body, offered today.

Inevitably, one has to name some less attractive old-fashioned habits which seem little reduced; such as the sense of class-divisions (as we saw, often transferred almost intact to new indicators of difference), brutalism and its cousin racism (listen to some football crowds for a mixture of those two). Some of these – for example, Saturday night drunkenness – are of very long standing; obviously they have increased with the increase of free money. And, usually under the urge to feed a drug addiction, so have muggings in the streets.

Two weeks ago, a widow of ninety-one was struck down and robbed in daylight on a narrow path near here by a young white man. The district is a mixture of lower-middle to middle-class people of all ages, with a complement of professionals using it as a first staging-post. The police told us they had logged well over thirty such incidents across these streets in the last few months. They had caught one young man, a heroin addict, who confessed to seven of those crimes.

Critical Literacy and Imaginative Literacy

Back to more general but fundamental questions. There are several kinds of literacy, such as: basic literacy; functional literacy; vocational literacy; and professional literacy. All are given their places today. All are relatively simple compared with two other kinds, to which we at present hardly give house-room; critical literacy and imaginative literacy.

As many as possible of the citizens of a potential democracy must be not only literate but critically literate – obviously, if they are to behave as full citizens. But the moment one says that one realises that critical literacy is not enough, is too negative, too rubbish-clearing. The next essential step must be towards a more civilized, cultivated, above all imaginative way of life; and one essential gateway to that is through the arts, and especially through good literature. A more important gateway is our experience of and from others, who embody those qualities; if we learn to recognize them.

If that sounds both academic, too prescriptive and like a filler of almost universal gaps one has to go on to say that it implies no undervaluing of 'ordinary' people. It recognizes hidden, actual and possible gifts in many. Beginning with what one might call that useful protective inertia; which can carry the ability to see through a false invitation and so to refuse to pick up some offered social and other changes, but especially the ideological and political. That quality is fed by irony and a range of bullshit detectors against phoney rhetoric. Then deep habitual roots can be drawn on, that resistance and resilience, that cocking of snooks, bloody-mindedness, biting of every proffered coin at least three times. Such protective attitudes are bedded in English working-class culture even more, it sometimes seem, than elsewhere. Favourite phrasings carry that network of responses: 'come off it'; 'he's not easily taken in'; 'he's got his head screwed on the right way'; and 'pull the other one – it's got bells on it'. It is all recognized and summed up generally as 'having a bit of common-sense'. And it all works to some extent against the pressure to lower our sights, that pressure so insidious that it feels as it tries to surround us, like a phoney eiderdown, made of polyfiller.

To approach from another angle: one also remembers here shrewd observations by C. S. Lewis and George Orwell. Both were looking at some of the material for reading directed at working-class people of their time; and, presumably, at other groups, to judge by the large sales. These could from one angle be called trash, repetitive, routine, predictable. One could also conclude, both of those authors saw, that underneath and chiefly implicitly, such books and magazines could invoke values which were in themselves not at all to be mocked or discredited. They dealt in credibilities which were not derisory, such as loyalty, affection, neighbourliness and kindness, and showed up the inadequacy of their opposites. There are a far cry from later sex-and-violence novels and their current successors; they belong to different worlds. It would be easy to romanticise such insights; but before that point is reached, they can point to worthwhile attitudes, hidden guides to behaviour; or at the very least attitudes to be recognized, not under-valued. Catherine Cookson's novels are impressive examples of that truth. Trollope has a sentence recognizing it. Of Marie Melmotte he finely says: 'The books she read, poor though they generally were, left something bright on her imagination'; which recalls Gide's perhaps equivocal remark in a letter to Mauriac: 'Bad literature is written with beautiful sentiments.'

A similar response may be made to music. Since I first heard it, I have been moved by M. Triquet's song of adoring homage to Tatyana in *Eugene Onegin*. Some time ago I read a music critic who said the song was of course sloppily sentimental and meant as parody [rather like Joyce's passage about the lame girl on the beach in *Ulysses*].

As to critical literacy and its place in schools, a good starting point is an observation by the American philosopher of education, John Dewey: 'What the best and wisest parent wants for his own child . . . the community must want for all its children.' How true, and how very unlike English practice.

Critical literacy should be part of every curriculum after, say, the age of eight. We may thus help pupils better to avoid the false communication traps all about us. To that process from the beginning the best aid is, yet again, reading; reading to the class and by the class. Not surprisingly, children who have been read to at home have been shown to have an advantage in class; and that requires teachers to do their best to bring the others along towards that level; which is not only functional. From that, one moves to critical literacy

The decision to introduce that will not go unchallenged. Too much is invested in unscrupulous approaches, which critical literacy will undermine, for it to have an easy passage. Some years ago, the education officer employed (in accordance with the Act then current) by a commercial television company to devise worthwhile programmes for schools, proposed a series on 'How to Read Advertisements'. The series was a useful basic introduction to critical literacy. The education officer was intelligent and well-informed; but, as it proved, naive about the commercial world. That reacted violently. The television company, whose profits of course depended on advertising, sacked the education officer once the pilot programme had been previewed, with outraged advertising executives in attendance. Watching television at home on the evening of the ruckus, the education officer saw his own job advertised, without having been himself told that he was sacked. When he nevertheless arrived for work the next day the personal belongings from his office were stacked in the foyer, his office locked against him; and a note delivered requiring him to hand in at once his office key and company credit card. They mean business, those people; for them, that kind of action is indeed justifiable; in the real world. Another of those forms of censorship which the mass society practises effortlessly.

Critical literacy is needed but subordinate to imaginative literacy. That should be encouraged from the start of school, at present from age five. It is the introduction to what Matthew Arnold, to quote him again, called 'the best that has been known and said'. 'And made', we might add, so as to bring in music and the visual arts. Becoming acquainted with these things at any level will not necessarily make us better citizens or better human beings. We may say that it stands available, if we so will; and if we approach it dispassionately, for itself.

Today, these claims will be unacceptable not only to people who are under-educated but also to most of those in positions of power and authority. Such legacies are not known about, or are ignored as 'irrelevant to modern living'. Most do not know of our past; it does not feed them, does not flow through their mental pathways. They make do in their scarce spare time with television's recreational re-creatings and visits to heritage sites. Or with the latest bestsellers when on holiday. You could not talk to them of Lawrence or Forster or Greene. Yeats, Eliot and Auden remain in an even more securely closed box. They feel no regret or sense of missing something. They know little of the foundations of their civilisation; for them it is not a civilization but a place, a market, with which constantly to engage, usually and simply for financial gain or greater public repute and the honours which can go with that. Still, there may be a Marie Melmotte hidden inside some of them, awakened by those occasional bestsellers. Or a Charles Darwin who, late in life, regretted the loss of his acute delight in poetry, Shakespeare, pictures, music; or a John Stuart Mill, who had similar regrets. 'Great art', said Iris Murdoch, 'is a selfless gazing at and recording of *what is there.*'

It is difficult, though, to be generous to some of those who have had ample opportunities to become acquainted with, let us say, the literary heritage. To those teachers, for instance, who seek to discard in schools all writing before 1900, on the ground that it is 'not relevant'. That word is widely subverted to mean anything which represents the latest literary fashion; its use then a mark of the uncivilized.

Cultural Institutions Questioned

Institutions of various types of further education, between sixth form and universities, are of all educational places the most heavily affected by the 'nothing like leather' vocational stress. Some of them are today sad places; they have many devoted staff, but some principals (or whatever P. R.-style names they have allotted themselves to go with their big car and big salary) act as though they are chief executives with a mission statement, designed in adspeak by their public relations office, to express their thoroughly vocational-functional purposes. Of all main types of educational institutions, many lecturers there are having the hardest time and need most outside help, beginning with improved salaries. They do not receive many guiding lights from above, from the universities; they would all in all not expect to do so. Nor do many universities recognize anything like an organic link, either (though a functional link is sometimes made).

Many universities are also rather dispirited places. Student numbers have gone up without concomitant increases in staff; salaries are by now lower than they used to be, in relation to those in other professions usually thought comparable (in 2002, a first year teacher in a junior school earned almost as much as some new university assistant lecturers, who may well have Ph.Ds), the stress on research has been increased and formalized to a degree which does truly suggest 'publish and be damned', and which can inhibit the right pace of enquiry. So has the approach to teaching itself. In the early days of these changes, one philosophy department entered, under the 'research' heading of the required report, a weekly discussion for staff members in the university sauna, devoted to 'advancing philosophy'; they were making a useful point.

It is hard for those of us who have for years been objecting to the small percentage who go on to university education to object here. After all, haven't we achieved what we sought? Not exactly. That expansion has been concurrent with those other changes named above, and those are making it difficult for universities and especially for the humanities within them, to operate successfully.

It is not so for those subjects which obviously have vocational-functional purposes. In universities they are likely, as elsewhere in education, to be given excessive pride of place. To some extent this was also true thirty years ago, in some universities; the representatives of the big sciences and big technologies were allowed to assume that they were in the front rank, and so would be particularly handsomely treated. This attitude is more widespread today.

Staffing at the top changes to match. Thirty or forty years ago you might expect a vice chancellor or principal to be one of the 'Great and Good', a chairman of national committees, a proconsul. One can think, to name only a few of the dead, of Lindsay, Moberly, Fulton, the brothers Morris, Beveridge, Boyle, Franks, Maud, Wolfenden, James. Such a vice chancellor was on occasion reminded that he was *primus inter pares,* of professorial calibre himself and among his equals. Today he or she is likely to be younger and leaner, the executive type, one who knows how to handle and probably to acquire money, to coax the disbursers of money, private or public. Here, the heads of Oxbridge colleges join him, often with an advantage. The vice chancellor will be supported and surrounded by not only the more trusted among his deans but by yet another office for public relations (and he too will agree to their issuing mission statements thought suitable for their kind of work); and by an office for fundraising, which will have a suitably escapist title, such as Office of the Development Executive.

It has long been difficult to suggest that a university should be *more*, admirable and essential though these activities are, than simply a place: 'where teaching goes on in the atmosphere of research'. Some writers, but not a sufficient number, have over the decades, here from Newman to F. R. Leavis, argued for that other and, to them, higher purpose. In much of Europe the Chicago *Great Books Programme* was thought something of a joke. It does not come as a surprise, therefore, that today almost all books in English which claim, for universities, functions wider – and deeper, they would say – than precisely focused teaching-and-research at no matter how high a level, have come from America. That is part of the admirable openness of the American spirit, including in scholarship. One can easily imagine the snide remarks in an English senior common room at the idea of, let us say, compulsory courses in all departments on Great Democratic Ideas.

That does not invalidate the belief that universities ought, to quote Irving Howe again, to 'bear witness' and stand for 'a substantive social morality', to introduce their students to some important issues outside the boundaries of their departmental specialisms but relevant to them. If their members have well-trained and exceptionally gifted minds and if they are teaching young people with something of that kind of promise, it seems right – inescapable – that they should be asked to bring those minds to bear on the nature of their societies and so on the way their disciplines might best contribute to (not simply 'serve') them. Giving evidence before an OECD enquiry into French higher education, an enquiry inspired by the student uprisings of the late-1960s, one very angry Professor, his voice rising through-out, reiterated again and again that his sole duty was to teach '*mes cours, mes cours*'. Perhaps he did that very well indeed; but if all professors shared his convictions, I am arguing, the universities would be more narrow minded than would be good for them, and for society. Some are. But the first questions for them, as they take breath from their scientific and technical work at the fron-tiers should, be: 'Who is going to use these findings? And to what purpose?'

Those questions are fair and inescapable. They do not suggest that students should be given ideologies, that teachers should be proselytizers. There are better ways of presenting such issues and their implications. But, properly examined, they would do much to alter for the good the atmosphere within which training is given in what are obviously socially important disciplines. Some subjects, in particular the humanities and social sciences, will almost inevitably go beyond the more directly vocational ones. A distinguished American professor of philosophy used to say that one of his functions was to put a maggot into the soft cheese of American society; that that was a proper function for him, as a philosopher. Not surprisingly, some of the best teachers within British universities' Schools of Extra-Mural Studies aimed to make those connections, from the turn to the twentieth century, in their two-hour tutorial classes. In making their own dispositions the universities today might learn from that instance, starting with considering the practice of R. H. Tawney in such classes.

Put simply and economically, in education today the stress on vocationalism at all levels has become so great that the word 'education' itself now often seems simply a synonym for training. No sensible person would wish the training of a potential heart-surgeon to be weakened so as to make room for an introduction to more general issues. But room can always be made for a good idea. If that training were in the round, deeply considered, integral, the heart surgery need not suffer; the surgeons' ability to understand the social, political and financial constraints under which their work was being done would be better informed and that would be for the good of all. They would not be assumed to be willing simply to accept their society, including – especially today – their not asking questions about the justification for a bifurcated NHS. It may be that something of this sort is included in some medical school training; one is bound to wonder, though, how searching it is since the medical profession taken as a whole remains conservative and defensive.

There enters here an institution whose role is to inform and enrich us as individuals, as families and as students of all kinds: the public libraries. They were founded in Britain a century and a half ago and have a magnificent record in opening horizons for whoever entered them. Hunslet gained its first public library during my adolescence and for me, as for very many others from bookless homes, that made an irreplaceable adjunct to our education.

It would be wrong to suggest that their staffs today are less well-motivated than any of their predecessors; but many are suffering from an uncertainty of purpose, or an inadequately-considered new purpose. Information technology is gaining ground so quickly and making ever more demands on funds (at a time when many local authorities, looking everywhere for places to make cuts, turn to the libraries as fairly easy victims). So staff too begin – in that horrible word – to 'prioritize' acquisitions in information technology, at the expense of books. But a library is nothing, has forsaken its main purpose, if it reduces its commitments to good books in and for themselves. Here, there really is nothing like leather. Nothing – no audio or video tapes, no screens or scanners or whatever other new invention within information processing – can take the place of an individual at whatever age sitting quietly absorbing the words on the pages of a good book, holding it, smelling it, running his hands over it, feeling its age. A good book really may be just as described by Milton: 'The precious life-blood of a master spirit, embalmed and treasured up to a life beyond life.' Carlyle echoed that 'a good book is the purest essence of a human soul', which cannot be replaced by any sophisticated devices or transpositions. Ideally, a good book has to be read, in itself, by one person, intensely quiet, absorbed. Then may 'the precious life-blood', 'the purest essence', be best tapped.

The phrase used just above – 'a good book' – must be carefully chosen today. Many librarians' uncertainly and uneasiness of purpose has led them to continue to buy at least some printed books; such as multiple copies of each month's bestsellers but none or one, to take an example of which I had direct experience some years ago, of a new book by the late Iris Murdoch. A weak justification for buying bestsellers is: 'If we persuade them to come inside to borrow a bestseller, they will be encouraged to go on to "serious" authors.' They will not. We are once again with the carousel and the escalator.

The British Council's Libraries across the world have introduced many thousands to the richness of British literature and so to that of British culture and society. An Indian scholar said to me, 'We can get Information Technology from almost anywhere, and indeed we are so advanced ourselves that we hardly need it from outside. Only you can give us Shakespeare'. It is hard to conceive of the thinking which has led recently to the council's disposing of books in its libraries – including the outstanding one in Paris – in favour of the tools of information technology. There is a direct line to this unimaginative decision from a debate about twenty years ago, when some in the council argued for teaching of the language to have clear pre-eminence over the presentation of English literature.

The libraries' difficulties have a direct impact on authors. Public libraries used to buy over a thousand copies of a well-received book, which did not necessarily mean a bestseller. That was an essential bedrock of sales for good books which were not likely to enter a bestseller list. Those library sales have now fallen to only a few hundred. For this and other reasons, many publishers have therefore become unwilling to accept such books; their total sales might not cover production costs. Do most public librarians realise what damage they are doing?

Here appears yet another and interlocking element, which concerns publishers and booksellers. Publishers are more and more consolidating into large groups which, they correctly claim, can produce economies of scale. They also produce managing bodies which concentrate on 'the bottom line', which are constantly looking for the possible bestseller; many of them do not have that love of books of all kinds and in themselves, which used to make British publishing so varied and such a support to authors, emerging or established. Several authors have told me in the last few years that their usual publishers, who nourished and had regularly accepted their work, have now been absorbed in a conglomerate and have written to say that they are no longer able to publish them. They did not explicitly say that the author's books would not break even; they well might have. But enough profit (in the accountant's eyes) could no longer be made from that kind of book; 'working-class' and 'Northern' novels are two examples. On the other hand a few publishers, it is said, still subsidise loss-making poetry from the profits of better sellers.

One publisher called popular novelists his 'assembly-line workers'; a woman author was told to cut much of the description in her novel: 'we have certain regulations about how much description you can put in'; others are asked to write directly to a formula.

The next step has been for the major bookselling chains to reach agreements with major publishers to give favourable discounts to them, in return for large and prominent display space; both not available to the smaller publishers. Books which challenge the reader will yield to sure blockbusters; the publishing and the bookselling trade, except for the small ones in each area, are losing the sense of books as a more than commercial product.

In response, Radio 4's 'You and Yours' programme announced that it would examine the process, but did a half-way job by concentrating almost wholly on the booksellers. Since the changes concern the publishers at least as much as the booksellers, are a continuous movement between the two, Radio 4's attention was like professing to examine dying flowers without looking at their roots.

It seems as though we are moving towards small circulations from small houses for books which do not have immediate commercial promise; writing such books and the circulation of them will revert to a hedge-industry, as it was across much of Europe in politically controlled times. There's progress for you, and in a democracy. At least the word-processor and the desk-top will save us from almost complete oblivion.

Last, in this list of what should be institutional aids to democratic involvement, there is broadcasting in the public service. But perhaps enough has already been said about that. To some extent most channels, but especially and rightly those of the BBC, do something to encourage democratic thinking and action. The main need, as was argued earlier, is to avoid putting such programmes into their own ghettos whilst providing dumbed-down programmes for larger audiences; these last as always being defended in the taken-in-vain name of democracy.

The Literary 'Happy Family'; Intellectuals Questioned

In bringing intellectuals into this debate one is on even trickier ground. Most British intellectuals, for mainly good reasons, shy away from any suggestion that they should 'engage with . . . advise' others who are not intellectuals. The word 'intellectual' is regarded by many intellectuals themselves with some suspicion and shrugged off, as though a dubious decoration was being offered, or an invitation to join the ranks of self-important European 'clerks', or of earnest Workers' Educational Association tutors. This attitude was (is?) also held by some arts council officials.

At such moments one realizes how far we have come from important nineteenth-century attitudes towards 'the education of the people'. Still, today's attitudes are understandable; if inadequate. Well-informed people write virtually for their own kind only, for their journals, and sometimes for the broadsheet newspapers. They leave those not so well informed to the often dubious embrace of the tabloids whether of the Right or the Left; and those reek of the *parti pris*. So one talks within one's own intellectual group and becomes a member of 'the chattering classes', or of Auden's 'literary happy family' and those labels imply that they do little but chatter rather than act. They seem cliquish. There are exceptions, of course; but one can fairly say that more British intellectuals put up their flags in defence of – admittedly, often flagrant – abuses in foreign lands than examine and judge less easily identified abuses at home.

So they often adopt a flippant style and advise anyone who talks of these home-grown abuses not to 'get hot under the collar'. Or they adopt a would-be lowbrow togetherness: 'well, if they like that sort of thing, who are we . . .'; or they are amused by even the most egregious advertisement: 'terribly well-made, and witty too'. (What do they expect? Many ads cost more than the programmes they interrupt.) Any twist or turn will do if one is to avoid seeming 'judgemental'; at just the point where an intelligent person *should* be judgemental. A parochial treason of the clerks.

Isaiah Berlin writes eloquently on the 'wholeness' of the Russian intellectual tradition, and of the 'moral charm' of the Russian intelligentsia – that last a splendid expression, but one which suggests a link strange to English ears. There comes to mind here also Tchekov's loving but stern injunction to his compatriots: 'You live badly, my friends. It is shameful to live like that.'

I do not urge British intellectuals to take to the streets frequently; but, sometimes, yes; and when they do respond, it should not always be to ills in distant lands or to the more fashionable among home-grown causes. Some important causes here are less evident; and taking to the streets not always the best way to help them.

Nor need intellectuals – writers and others – be alone in defending causes. There are still many institutions and voluntary bodies who could on the right occasions make common cause with them. The political parties and trade unions could be urged to widen their vision so that they take in social causes not always evidently or immediately related to success in more narrow and obvious terms. Some years ago Australian trade unions struck to avoid a fine stand of trees in the middle of a big and expanding city from being felled by developers.

Even more directly to the point, but at present little addressed or recruited to social action, are those who enrol in adult education classes, in the evenings and at weekends. There are estimated to be about a million of them. Naturally not all would respond by practical action to a social or political issue which they wished, by study, to understand better. Many enrol in adult classes (not for vocational purposes; those are counted within further education) simply out of intellectual interest, to learn about subjects which have little if any easily discernible social or political relevance; at least, may have seemed to have that outlook, before they began to study. Many others in that million do have or acquire such interests, and these usually determine their choice of subject. Towards the end of its life the national Advisory Council for Adult and Continuing Education made a survey which included asking respondents what led them to join classes. A substantial number gave answers of the sort: 'so as to understand myself/other people/society better'. It seems as though there are many Jude the Obscures, or Leonard Basts or Anxious Corporals or members of Arnold's 'Saving Remnant', still seeking knowledge and understanding today 'for the love of God and the relief of man's estate'. Their earnestness is easily mocked; it would be better if more intellectuals gave them support – in, as objectively as possible and for a start, helping them to enlarge their abilities to handle knowledge and understand its implications.

Some Things to Do

Finally, some practical moves towards improving civil society; some are small and some will seem unattractive; but all deserve consideration.

We have to accept the need for more democratic legislation, often adopted against the odds and against the predictable voices professing to speak for democratic freedom, and claiming that 'the market' can always be left to regulate itself. A false argument. Regulations are needed in any society, obviously and in small as well as large matters. They are essential to 'open capitalist democracies'.

Notably, rules are essential, as was argued before, in the way we set up and monitor broadcasting. So is a Press Complaints Commission, but one exercising powers which can deter. The *British Journalism Review* speaks admirably for responsible journalism, but that voice is not sufficient to prevent today's more flagrant misdemeanours. We have trading standard officers, usually under-funded. Advertising, too, has its own supervisory committee but seems not to frighten that body of practitioners. These sorts of body often seem like the misbehaved judging the misbehaving. One could add many more such evident needs.

Which leads to the most tendentious and difficult types of legislation: those which attempt to restrain what come to be considered undesirable *attitudes* in some, perhaps many, citizens; on, for example, such matters as capital punishment and racism. The last survey of which I know showed a majority in favour of capital punishment; similarly, it is thought that a majority still harbour racist attitudes.

One of the favourite shibboleths of the time is that a referendum is indisputably and always a very good thing, which should be resorted to on every possible occasion and its results accepted; once more in the name of democracy. Paradoxically, one secretary of state described Gibraltar's call for a referendum on her future as 'short-circuiting the democratic process'. Yet referenda on each of those two issues named above would run against present legislation. Parliament has passed laws against both, has here apparently gone against the common will. Has Parliament therefore acted undemocratically? If you believe in the sovereign, the over-riding, power of the referendum, yes. Otherwise you have to believe that occasionally it is more democratic for Parliament to go against the common will by acting, if those elected members believe this to be right, in a more humane and civilized manner than would the majority of their constituents. One might well have expected that a 'Democratic Movement' demanding referenda on both those matters named above would have arisen. The fact that such acts were passed without formal reference to a national count, but were not massively challenged in reaction to them, may be a sign of inanition, or an indication that we are still if slowly moving towards that better democratic condition.

That seems unlikely. In late 2002 a dispute arose over the way Lottery funds were allotted to good causes. Some argued that the only 'democratic' way would be for buyers of tickets to indicate in advance which causes they thought should benefit. Very, very few of us have much knowledge of the huge range and purposes of British charities. The democratic way of deciding is to ask a group of well-informed people (not public stuffed turkeys) to do that job for the rest of us.

This may be the point at which to introduce some cheerful public initiatives, which were founded or have important centres in Britain, such as: PEN, Oxfam, Amnesty, Charter 88, Index on Censorship, VLV (Voice of the Listener and Viewer), among several others. Victims of famine, of abuses of human rights, of savage censorship, of torture and many other atrocities have cause to be grateful for voluntary organizations such as those; here and elsewhere, of course.

A somewhat similar issue has also recently emerged, to unusually vigorous attention: the constitution of the reformed House of Lords. There is a dispute as to how many non-elected members there might be. Many people believe, predictably in the name of democracy, that it should be wholly elected. To that, the other side argues that such a composition would not be sufficiently different from that of the House of Commons, being also wholly elected and so directly responsive to those who elected them, whoever they might be.

This brings up the basic question: what is the purpose of a second chamber? To provide useful but not overriding checks-and-balances on the House of Commons, those on both sides of the argument may reply. A practical but not profound justification.

But aren't even elected members likely to be often place-men and -women, old fogeys, hoisted into position because they have friends in the right places, members of the Establishment, and so on? Not, their supporters reply, if they are elected through new forms of constituency rather as members of the European Parliament are? For several reasons, from social, through structural to geographic and further, that is not a good example.

I have not heard a further argument for non-elected members;

one which might be called the Cincinnatus Case. There are without doubt many people highly qualified in the various issues which come before Lords and Commons, people more qualified than most now in those places. By no means all would propose themselves for membership by election; they are busy and enjoy their work. But some might be persuaded to leave their ploughs and, for the public good, serve for a term in the Lords or a Senate. Some such people are already Life Peers and most of them exceptionally valuable (others are place-men and -women; the present selection system is full of such holes). To denigrate such people in favour of the elected, to insist that those not elected be a small minority, if any are appointed at all, is to reject the best help of many talented people, and to narrow the definition of 'democracy'.

The case for total election is at bottom vague and romantic. Paradoxically, it rests in part on suspicion of the House of Commons and sometimes of MPs in general. It believes nominations will almost always result in the naming of those already known to the Establishment. It has, by contrast, a vision of a House mainly staffed by 'ordinary people'; but who are they? Almost by definition, 'ordinary people' will be hardly known and have little if any experience of public responsibility. If they have that, they cease to be ordinary and join the ranks of those who may be suspected of being in some ingrown, influential group or other (councillors, magistrates and the like).

But the Cincinnatus Principle, of invitation on the grounds of qualifications, to people often not willing to stand for election, who would have to be persuaded to enter the Lords if asked – that principle is a good one. It takes the House of Lords further away from being a simulacrum of the Commons, not sufficiently different; and it reduces and, so long as it is very carefully worked out, may remove altogether the risk of non-elected members being merely friends or nominees of the conventionally mistrusted great and good. The wholly elected system has a similar weakness to that of the total commitment to referenda; except that, unlike referenda which may be thought likely to gain strength as democracy itself strengthens, the case for non-elected members to the Lords is strong from the start and will always remain so. There will always be valuable Cincinnatus's to be if possible tempted from that plough.

That issue leads to another with some similar characteristics and one also much discussed – or, rather, often dismissed out of hand nowadays. That is: whether Quangos (quasi-autonomous non-governmental organisations), such as Royal commissions, departmental committees and the like have any use, at any time. They are nowadays fashionably and routinely scorned as bodies staffed by those familiar stuffed birds, people chosen from equally routine lists of 'safe' personalities, who will compose committees which will decide only in the way the sitting government wishes, or produce some bland on-the-one-hand-on-the-other conclusions which leave governments free to do what they would have done anyway, without a committee; so they are, it is argued, face-savers and buyers of time. And, of course, undemocratic.

I have served (unpaid, of course) on four such national committees: respectively, on youth services, broadcasting, the arts and adult education. They had their longeurs, but all of them were strongly, even fiercely, mindful of their freedom from government. They were all in their time mocked or attacked by parts of the press; and by some members of Parliament or the Lords, if their proposals ran against the attackers' interests or opinions. They all tried honestly to make useful proposals for improvement, and dissenting annexes to their reports were rare even though the committees' compositions had always been carefully made representative of differing political and other interests. Each one's political interests were undeclared and most remained unknown. They knew that not all they recommended would be accepted; but tried not to trim what they proposed in the hope that it would be at least partially accepted. They all gave time which could have been used for other work – writing a book, for instance – but one did not hear anyone grumble about that. They happily gave more time than almost all MPs or Peers could spare if they were to look in depth at a precise issue and then hand their findings to those who had established them, knowing well that the degree to which their proposals would be accepted would depend not only on their validity as arguments but on many other considerations, starting with the political weather. Non-political national committees (notably Royal commissions and departmental committees) can be a useful instrument of a democracy; so long as they are established within the principles of democracy, not as politically loaded devices. Of those I served on, the Pilkington Committee on the Future of Broadcasting was the most taxing, in scope the most broad and bracing, and the most hated in some quarters – because it went against large financial interests (which were, naturally, called democratic interests). A proof of its force came when a wealthy man, financially interested in the establishment of commercial television, publicly burned the report in a garden bonfire, with like-minded friends in attendance. That was a kind of victory for a Quango.

There is much to do, big and small, to make this country even a marginally better democracy. Here is a more or less random list, but all its entries are important in different degrees.

Pay more attention to the needs of the underclass; help more comprehensives to work as well as do the best of them; put more public stress on good nutrition; be more suspicious of engaging in public-private partnerships, especially of major monopoly services; bear down more heavily on 'developers' and fiddling solicitors and accountants, large and small; establish the principle of corporate manslaughter; protect more firmly the principle of public service in broadcasting (it seems as though, by the time this is published, that principle will have been even further weakened by the opening of broadcasting franchises to foreign buyers); abolish or reform the honours system which is at present too much an unhealthy mixture of old-style time-servers and – especially recently – new-style and shamelessly populist idols, and so on.

To repeat: the last few pages are no more than a slight sketch of some actions which, in one person's view, might help towards the emergence of a real democracy, a more civil society. It rests, it must rest, on a guarded optimism. 'A man's reach must exceed his grasp; or what's a heaven for'; not towards a heaven perhaps, but neither to an authoritarian society nor a society of the massively and blindly persuaded, populated by the hinds of consumerism. Not a society of the totalitarianism of the Far Right or the Rigid Left, either, but an open society whose members are self-choosing; and so a place harder to live in than one in which people have allowed themselves to become the helots of the self-interested communicators of all kinds. An open society is always under threat precisely because it is so open, open to be subverted. But it remains more promising than any other form we know of or can at present envisage.

Many people will dismiss all I have said here; that such a response is built into the kind of society I have been describing, one of its prophylactics. To the more thoughtful I would, near the end, offer two observations I always enjoy quoting. Gotthold Lessing in the eighteenth century asserted: 'We must not accept the wantlessness [splendid word] of the poor.' That may counsel practical help for the 'underclass'. It may just as well refer to the inner condition of many of us, who are being taught to be spiritually wantless.

And in the early nineteenth century Bishop Wilson argued that: 'The number of those who need to be awakened is far greater than that of those who need comfort.' Today's Judes need comfort, certainly; but most of their numerous workmates are not even aware of what they are missing.

A final reminder from Coleridge, on the nature of democracy: 'It has never yet been seen, or clearly announced, that democracy, as such, is no proper element in the constitution of a state.

The idea of a state is undoubtedly a government . . . or autocracy. Democracy is the healthful lifeblood which circulates through the veins and arteries, which supports the system, but which ought never to appear externally, and as the mere blood itself.' As so much of Coleridge's prose, that is not easy to decipher. It is, I think, saying that democracy is, above and before all, a state of mind and will, from which a good system may emerge and by which it is supported. Without such a system, democracy is a structurally empty assertion. As so often today.

Final Words

Behind this final chapter, indeed (I now see) behind much of this book, is a huge unanswered question. In a time of increasing unbelief can we still find 'oughts', which will justify ethics, values, adherences outside the needs and wishes of the self? Incidentally, I do not think that space research need weaken the belief in God.

A Christian will object that to reduce Christianity (and most other religions) to a source of ethics for life-time behaviour is to denature it, not to recognize that a religion calls us to the acceptance of a life beyond life; that without that extra dimension even our ethics, having no source beyond and outside themselves, are contingent rules to save us from each other and from ourselves; desperate attempts to avoid a life 'nasty, brutish and short'. A friend adds: 'If you take ethics away from their religious roots they will become like cut flowers and eventually die'; and reminds me that Blake said: 'If morality was Christianity, Socrates was the Saviour.'

I can at the moment take this no further. It is of little comfort that better minds have wrestled with the question for centuries and not reached agreement. Still, that fact can also offer a kind of encouragement to some of us: to go on going on, asking and trying to arrive at more clarity, if not an 'answer'.

Index